A DIFFERENT VISION
A REVOLUTION AGAINST
RACISM IN PUBLIC EDUCATION

A DIFFERENT VISION

A Revolution Against
Racism in Public Education

Susan Anglada Bartley, M.Ed

LUMINARE PRESS
WWW.LUMINAREPRESS.COM

A Different Vision: A Revolution Against Racism in Public Education
© 2018 Susan Anglada Bartley, M.Ed

Printed in the United States of America

Luminare Press
438 Charnelton St., Suite 101
Eugene, OR 97401
www.luminarepress.com

LCCN: 2017964348
ISBN: 978-1-944733-50-6

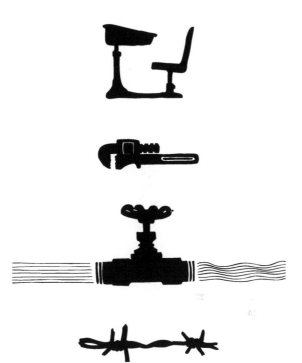

CONTENTS

What is normal is young people making mistakes. And we've got to be able to distinguish between dangerous individuals who need to be incapacitated and incarcerated versus young people who, in an environment in which they are adapting but if given different opportunities, a different vision of life, could be thriving the way we are.

–PRESIDENT BARACK OBAMA,
July 16, 2015, Remarks at El Reno Federal Penitentiary

*freedom now not in the afterlife
if I want to break free I have to fight
poverty death and slaughter, post-traumatic stress disorder
school-to-prison pipeline spend a lifetime just caught up*

–EXCERPT FROM "VILLAIN DOWN,"
2018, by Emcee, Educator, and Cultural Activist
Mic Crenshaw

*See my people stay alive by giving respect to the dead
police can't do their job without poppin' some meds
you aint gotta scrape old paint for kids to eat lead
but my granny kept us safe, shotgun under the bed.*

–EXCERPT FROM "COMMERCIAL FREE,"
2009, by Creative and Visual Artist
Edreys Wajed

ACKNOWLEDGEMENTS

Special thanks to the family of Paulo Freire and to Continuum, an imprint of Bloomsbury Publishing for granting explicit permission to quote his deeply inspirational work, *Pedagogy of the Oppressed*. © Paulo Freire, 1921, *Pedagogy of the Oppressed, Continuum*, an imprint of Bloomsbury Publishing Plc.

Thank you to authors Eduardo Bonilla-Silva, Ann Byrd, Barnett Berry, and Alan Wieder, journalists Emily DeRuy, Caitlin Emma, and Rebecca Klein, and architect, school building expert, and advocate Lindsay Baker for permission to refer to your work.

Thank you to Emcee, Educator, and Cultural Activist Mic Crenshaw and Creative and Visual Artist Edreys Wajed for permission to quote your lyrics.

Thank you to former Milwaukie Teacher's Union President Bob Peterson for permission to quote your work, *A Revitalized Teacher Union Movement*.

Thank you to the New Press for permission to refer to Dr. Michelle Alexander's work *The New Jim Crow*.

Thank you, fellow educators Shay James, Ivonne Dibblee, Lavert Robertson, Marshall Haskins, Chris Frazier, and Diallo Lewis for your relentless dedication to anti-racist philosophy and racial justice in public education.

Thank you to Bill Bigelow and Linda Christensen for your tremendous legacy of supporting culturally relevant teaching.

Thank you, Domingo Urrutia, Dorene Williams-Jones, William McClendon, Pamela Garrett, Trevor Butenhoff,

Marilyn Mi, Hoang Tran, Jeffrey McGee, Charles McKinney, Kim Amador, Mercedes Munoz, Courtney Palmer, and Gwen Sullivan for the battles we fought together.

Thank you, Kenneth Berry, Sheila Washington Warren, Ellis Leary, and Ron Herndon for your unceasing dedication to racial justice in public education in Portland, Oregon - your great faith is the light that guides my work.

Great thanks to Ali McCart at Indigo Editing, Independent Editor Lamarra Haynes, Creative and Visual Artist Edreys Wajed, and the entire team at Luminare Press.

Thank you, James Duggan. Never stop teaching.

Thank you, Professors Tricia Rose & Robin D.G. Kelley for flipping my world, and June Foley for seeing me.

Thank you, Jaime Marrero, Linda Weill, Judy Chambers for your friendship and support.

Thank you, mother, Maureen Bartley, for your relentless faith in humanity and for helping me to see the magic in each child. Thank you, father, John Bartley, for encouraging me to think critically. Thank you, brother, Aaron Bartley for the ways you strengthened me.

Thank you, educator, strategist, healer, friend, and husband Pedro Anglada Cordero, MSW for all of your love. Thank you, Simone, for giving me no choice other than hope.

Thank you, students, for all of the great lessons in faith.

IN MEMORIAM

This book is dedicated to the memory of
educator and professor

DR. CHARLES HOPSON
(12/17/1957 – 10/9/2012)
Rest in Power

&

to the memories of

FERNANDO CHAVEZ
(10-21-91 – 6-6-2009)
and
TERRY DONNELL ELLIOTT
(1-27-92 – 2-23-2009)

INTRODUCTION
Why We Must Fight

Long-standing issues of injustice in U.S. public schools require educators, parents, and community members to demand a revolution in our system of public education. Providing excellent, high-quality education to the millions of students of different ethnic groups and racial categories attending our public schools is not a problem or a chore; it is an opportunity to move past historical oppression, to move towards a new version of education that embraces the diverse cultural realities of the millions of students we serve. Anything less than a total revolution in how we approach education will continue the status quo that upholds systemic racism, and, moreover, the widely documented outcome that we have come to know as the school-to-prison pipeline.

To proceed, we must be willing to acknowledge that schools in the United States were founded to promote and maintain white supremacy. For some, this may be a harsh reality to accept, but many are aware that school integration and equal access to education were core issues in the battle for civil rights that took place in the 1950s and 60s. Segregated schools were loci of white supremacy, places where white power and white values derived from a Puritanical past were taught and proliferated. Imprinted into our collective cultural memory is the image of the courageous Ruby Bridges walking into a previously all-white school in 1960.

Her courage marked a moment when barriers were broken, when civil rights were achieved. In reality, Ms. Bridges only entered a labyrinth of institutionalized racism still needing deconstruction to be made viable for her community, and for hundreds of other non-white communities that yearned for access to that same dream of educational opportunity that was readily available for white children.

Today, many of us still work, live, and send our children into a system, founded in white supremacy, which *has never been fully deconstructed.* The rules have changed about who can attend, but the pedagogy and disciplinary practices remain deeply rooted in the same system of white supremacy, designed to promote and maintain racial segregation while propelling white children into the higher social stratosphere. Literature taught in schools has recently (in the past fifteen years and only in some schools) begun to include literature and history of marginalized communities in the United States. The battle to exclude the literature and history of marginalized communities in school curriculum has continued in the Arizona legislature into 2017. Arizona's exclusionary legislation is only one, very obvious example of white supremacy in public education. The manner in which students are disciplined, and the rate at which they attend college and take college prep courses also evidence the promotion of white supremacy. In addition to the discrimination, bias, humiliation, and rejection that many children of color have experienced, some also carry generational pain from the racist trauma their parents and/or grandparents underwent. Trusting *the system* has never been entirely beneficial for communities of color in the United States, and has often led to further trauma, as *the system* is designed to protect and promote white children and simultaneously neglect and condemn children of color. Until the racist disciplinary practices, curriculum, access to higher education, and the pain of racist trauma are addressed, the recognized cultural heritage, ideological foundation, and institutional policy of public education in the United States remains scripted by and in service of white people and white, Anglo-Americentric values.

Even in 2016, the vast majority of educators nation-wide were white, though public school students are increasingly non-white. A 2016 U.S. Department of Education study called *The State of Racial Diversity in the Educator Workforce* revealed that more than 82% of public school teachers are white, while students of color will make up more than 54% of the population of public schools by 2024. Since the system is largely managed and operated by whites, it becomes unconsciously and consciously aligned with values that support the continuation of white power and privilege, *even when it intends not to.*

Throughout the history of the discussion of race and education, many writers have discussed the *problem of race* or *the race problem.* One of the first was Alexander Crummell, who, coincidentally, first read his paper *The Race Problem in America* in 1889 at the Protestant Episcopal Church in my hometown of Buffalo, New York. Crummell, on the 12th page of his famous paper, comes upon an important thought, "Race-life is a permanent element in our system. Can it be maintained in peace?"

Crummell's haunting question is as valid today as it was in 1889. The resounding answer from Black and Brown activists is: *peace cannot be maintained without justice.* Moreover, the peace Crummell imagines has never been part of the reality experienced by Black, Latino, Asian, or

Native American people in the United States. He is correct, at least to this moment, in his description of race as a fixture, or permanent element, in our society. However, he fails to write much about the psychological and physical violence required to maintain racism. Racism is a perpetual violence that continues to be hard for many whites to see. It is a violence that is still here with us today, in our schools and prisons, in the fabric of our daily life, as ripe, pungent, and real as when Crummell posed his original question.

A few pages later, he writes:

> But just here the caste spirit interferes in this race-problem and declares: "You Negroes may get learning; you may get property; you may have your churches and your religion; but this is your limit! This is the white man's Government! No matter how many millions you may number, we Anglo-Saxons are to rule!" This is the edict constantly hissed in the Negro's ear, in one vast section of the land. (17)

Crummell, though he can be criticized for discussing race as a *problem* rather than viewing race as a source of great wealth for our nation, brought about some valuable questions that still do not have answers today. The murders of Black community members, including Reverend and Senator Clementa Pickney at Mother Emmanuel Baptist Church in South Carolina by a young white supremacist and the ensuing battle over the presence of the Confederate flag—the Civil War emblem of white power, demonstrate the continued relevance of Crummell's question and statement. The exclusion of Black and Brown children from education, starting in kindergarten and extending on up to higher education, also demonstrates the relevance of Crummell's question. One hundred and twenty-eight years later and children of color don't have the same rights as whites in society. Nationally, Black and Brown children still experience violent punishments, in the form of exclusion, economic disenfranchisement, and even imprisonment when they break the classroom and school rules that maintain white supremacy.

Racial demographics in the United States have changed drastically since 1889. No longer can issues related to race in education be polarized into Black and white. According to the Pew Research Center, who reported data from the U.S. Census Bureau, the U.S. "Hispanic" population grew to 53 million in 2012, a 50% increase since 2000 and nearly six times the population in 1970. Likewise, the U.S. Census Bureau reported significant increases in the numbers of Asian Americans between 2000 and 2010, which means even greater diversity, as these numbers represent growth in widely diverse Asian ethnic groups including Chinese, Filipino and Pacific Islander, Japanese, and Korean people. During this ten year period, California, New York, and Hawaii experienced the most substantial increase in the Asian American population with smaller increases in other states.

The following statement from the population research organization, ESRI further highlights the nation's changing racial demographics:

> If current rates of population change trend as they have for the past 20 years, by 2035, non-Hispanic whites will be outnumbered by minorities. In fact, Hawaii, California, New Mexico, and Texas have minority non-Hispanic white populations today.

The ESRI report also states:

As many know, the minority with the largest population increase between 2000 and 2010 was Hispanics, growing by 15.2 million people, or 43 percent. The black and Asian populations each increased by more than 4 million, with growth rates of 12.3 percent and 43.3 percent respectively. Multiracial Americans are a growing part of the demographic landscape, increasing from 1.4 percent to 2.9 percent of the population from 1990 to 2010, and today represent the fastest-growing population (45.9 percent) under age 18. Multiracial Americans are expected to reach 3.31 percent of the population by 2017.

It is time to stop looking at race as a problem. Race and changing racial demographics do present a challenge to white supremacy. White people who have relied on public institutions to continue to promote white power in society will continue to view shifting racial demographics as a problem. Those who understand that the new America will require a transformation from its racist past will embrace the opportunity to revolutionize our schools and public institutions. It is time to examine how we, a workforce of educators that is 82% white, can examine our school populations and develop a set of pedagogical frameworks that genuinely serve the students. We must scrutinize the methodologies used to discipline students, carefully extracting exclusion, humiliation, and supremacy from our schools. We must create a system that adults from diverse communities feel comfortable working in so that students see themselves represented in their learning environments, and so that these indispensable educators of color can act as transformers of our system and guardians of the values they will share and implement.

In writing this book, I have often asked myself if people will believe that a white woman who lives in Portland, Oregon, the whitest major city in the United States, could write a valuable book about racial justice in education. I ask you to consider that I began my service as an educator at the start of a ten year period in which the Hispanic population in Portland, Oregon exploded. According to a USA Today report, the Hispanic population in Portland grew 64% between 2000 and 2010. The Oregonian also reported a 44% growth in the Asian population in 2010 and a 22% increase in its Black population. Upon entering the school environment, I noticed rampant racism in school policies, athletics, and discipline. Portland's whiteness does not exempt it from racism; in fact, white supremacy is easier to promote and maintain when the great majority of leaders, school leaders, and active parents are white. The dynamics in Portland are very similar to the dynamics in hundreds of thousands of semi-urban and suburban districts that are, as of late, receiving influxes of students of color (and struggling to meet their needs).

Under the mentorship of the late revolutionary Principal Dr. Charles Hopson, an Afrocentric scholar and professor at the University of Portland, I had the opportunity to participate in many closed-door conversations about the dynamics of racism as they presented themselves at the school and throughout the district. I can now see that he used me as a foot soldier in a war that he had been fighting all of his life. He asked me to work with the district grant writer to apply for a 2.5 million dollar Federal SLC-

PREP grant that was funded by the Gates Organization. After securing the grant, Dr. Hopson placed my colleague Pamela Garrett and I at the helm of the project, ensuring that we had the authority to spend the money in a way that would promote equity and college preparation for all students.

Dr. Hopson departed for a position at the District Office, and another outstanding African American principal, Shay James, succeeded him. Principal James, a good friend and fellow mentee of Dr. Hopson, encouraged me to continue the work of developing innovative teaching strategies that were designed to promote access to college for all students. Under the leadership of both of these amazing individuals, I worked with a small group of colleagues to develop the Franklin High School Advanced Scholar Program. The equity-focused program required students to take a minimum of four AP courses or three AP courses and one Dual Credit course and provided students with a teacher mentor to help them on the path to higher education. Between 2008 and 2016, the number of students taking on this challenge grew from 88 to 465, with teacher mentors going above and beyond to mentor students, 100% of program participants were accepted to college or community college between 2012-2016. Franklin had the highest graduation rate for African American students in the state of Oregon in 2014, with increasing rates for students of Latin American heritage as well. For my leadership in dramatically increasing the number of students of color and students living in poverty taking AP and Dual Credit courses, I was awarded the *National Education Association's* H. Councill Trenholm Human and Civil Rights Award in 2012, the *OnPoint Community Credit Union* Excellence in Education Award in 2014, and the *Portland Public Schools* Outstanding Achievement Award in 2014.

The reality is, however, that even at Franklin High School, where many teachers accepted and embraced some radical changes, racism and exclusionary practices remain. The work is not done. So I write this book as a white educator who is ready to say that the problem is me. The problem is us—the 82%. We have to look at every aspect of our pedagogical and institutional practices. We have to examine our school populations to understand exactly who we are serving. We have to ask ourselves if we are creating a work environment where Black, Latino, and Native American staff members feel comfortable. We have to dismantle a discipline system that has, for decades, fed students of color into the school-to-prison pipeline. We have to be willing to continue to change. This book is about how. In reading it, I invite you to come with me on a journey toward a lofty dream that Dr. Martin Luther King, Reverend Clementa Pickney, and many others lost their lives for. Why, in the era of Betsy DeVos, should we still believe their dream is possible? If we truly love our students and our country, we have no choice but to continue to fight for a more just society.

While the premise of the book discusses the explosion of several populations, I acknowledge these changing demographics to highlight the shifting landscape of U.S. schools. I do not mention it to promote an ideology of multiculturalism. I do not subscribe to the melting pot theory. There are many problems with the melting pot theory. One being that history shows us it is more common for marginalized communities to remain intact and never fully integrate into the whole due to a combination of gatekeeping, marginalization, and the choice to stay together. Another being that cultural identity and heritage are not substances that we should wish to melt, break down. The idea of being melted sounds like a form of torture that would cause immense pain—and it does. Our white supremacist educational system boils students of color into capitulation by commanding them to bow down to a system that does not promote their interests. In this light, schools could be compared to kettles or melting pots, and educators profiteers who thrive on the homogenization of children, throwing students who don't fit into the prisons after failing to boil them into submission.

Heroic educators and education reformers like Pedro Noguera and Michelle Alexander have described this horrible reality. These writers walked the walk, survived the system, did the research, and lived to analyze and critique racism within the system with hawkish precision. They are not public school teachers who are currently in the trenches, but their hearts are. Reading their work gave me insight that unquestionably impacted my teaching. It also fed the part of my soul that needed allies in this work. Reading their work (if you already haven't) will help you to understand the national problems that are endemic in the U.S. public school system—so that you can see that the challenges your students encounter daily are challenges that an entire nation of students is also facing.

Namely, both authors write about the practice of **exclusionary discipline**—the national, systematic method of excluding students of color at far higher rates than white students. Exclusionary discipline can include requiring a student to leave the learning environment for a short period during class or excluding students from learning for weeks or months as a form of punishment for a violation, misunderstanding, or an accusation from a teacher or school official. This practice is harmful both because of the proven targeting of students of color and because it causes inequity in the actual exposure to classroom learning that students receive. Asking questions about how exclusionary discipline is happening in your school and district is an action that you can take to begin or push forward the work of deconstructing racism in public education. The only way we will solve this problem is if more teachers, new and veteran, are willing to raise their voices and challenge exclusionary discipline practices—but we must also refuse to exclude students from our classrooms. It is also essential to have knowledge of the U.S. prison system and enter teaching with an awareness of the ethnic/racial demographics of the corrections system in your state. Alexander's book, *The New Jim Crow*, will provide the information you need to gain a well-informed perspective on the school-to-prison pipeline.

After informing ourselves, educators must familiarize ourselves with the specific populations we serve and sincerely understand which populations are increasing at the highest rates. Regardless of your ethnic background, you can join the fight against racism in public education. Align yourself with those who have dedicated their lives to combatting white supremacy and racism. Continue reading this book for more strategies that you can employ in your classroom or suggest in your community to build more positive relationships with students of color and stop the cycle of marginalization and exclusion. I invite you to join those of us who are teachers and activists, and *also* healers of the pain inflicted by white supremacy and its offspring—racism, classism, and gender identity discrimination.

If you wish to do this work, the good news is that you are not alone. There are millions of educators who are eager to work with like-minded, equity-focused peers. There is a paradox at work—those who desire to transform the system must speak up against the status quo to find other like-minded folks, yet doing so requires courage and silent submission is always encouraged in hierarchical systems. Observe the quiet apathy present in staff meetings and professional development sessions. Often, those who are vocal are dealing with issues related to workload, scheduling, or other organizational concerns. Equity is not a priority unless administrators, counselors, teachers, and parents, or alumni make it a priority. Someone has to say *we are putting the discussion and the action about equity before the discussion about the radiator in room 160.*

I am writing this after school in a room that has had no heat all winter long. I could have spent the entire year complaining about it, but there was a simpler solution— wear a sweater and focus my energy on what matters more. Otherwise, there will always be something in the way. This doesn't mean I don't report the problem; I want my students to be warm just as much as the next teacher. Of course, I put in a call to facilities and ask for a solution. My point is that in an underfunded educational system there will always be 99 problems, from the copy machine to the broken window; *children with broken hearts and undiscovered brilliance must matter more.*

PART I

Accepting Responsibility

This book will be useful for teachers, school counselors, administrators, district leaders, graduate professors, policymakers, and community activists who desire to reflect on the current status of classroom instruction and school systems in efforts to move beyond the racist structure and implement a new system that works for all young people.

As non-white populations swell nationally, and neighborhoods that were previously home to specific ethnic populations are gentrified causing dispersal of people of color to new school communities that were previously majority white, all educators and community members will need to face the truth—our system is the problem. Let's solve it.

To absolve our educational system of its deeply entrenched racism, we must take the time to envision how a genuinely equitable system will look. How will it function, who will be in charge, how will it be funded? We know that teams constituted of 82% white educators cannot be in charge of this vision. The envisioning process must include constituents of color who are directly from the communities in need of transformation. Having "input" from people of color analyzed by predominantly white boards of directors, school administrators, parents, or teacher teams will not work. The necessary transformation will require that leaders and community members of color communicate how they would like to see the system of education reformed, with the faith that their ideas will be enacted immediately without backpedaling or excuse-making. This process doesn't mean that the role of white educators in public education is obsolete; it *means* that white educators need to become active listeners and take a service-oriented position, instead of assuming we have the right to collect and filter the comments of people of color.

All powerful systems, unchecked, will ultimately attempt to keep moving forward as they are, only making crucial changes if threatened. We, as white educators, have proven that (even with the very best intentions) we cannot be trusted to make decisions that fully benefit youth of color. We, as educators of all backgrounds, must participate in a creative visioning process that does not subjugate, silence, or filter the voices of our staff members of color. The new vision will require a set of fearless leaders of color and white supporters who are willing to speak up without fear or repercussions, who are empowered with the same financial support, creative freedom, and confidence as white predecessors who have failed.

White educators and community members can play an invaluable role by championing our excellent colleagues and leaders of color. White educators must reject the exclusion and silencing of our colleagues and leaders of color. Support them when they voice unpopular opinions, ask how we can take some of the heat, and show enough humility to attempt to work with the solutions they provide. While this may feel, for some whites, like taking an unfair step back in regards to professional success, the success and survival of our children and our public education system as a whole must be of more value than personal success.

As a whole community, including all who live in this society, we must examine every facet of our institutions, working to dismantle and rebuild with an entirely different vision. Let's begin with an examination of the ways in which the current approach to discipline in U.S. schools leads to obscene rates of imprisonment for people of color. Then, let's accept the responsibility of seeing and removing inequity in every aspect of our system. We must take the time to investigate how our accepted methods of disciplining and educating young people engender racism and poverty. We must consider how the diseased structures that hold our youth, at the macro and micro level, generate inequity. We must accept that, nationally, we are already living in a state of crisis concerning human rights. It is already too late to turn back. The only way is forward.

1

The Landscaping of White Supremacy in US Public Schools

Dear _____,

I still remember the way that you entered my classroom like you owned it back in the 9th grade. I could see your comedic brilliance and theatrical creativity as soon as you entered the room. Your presentation of the puppet theater version of Oedipus Rex in which you gave all of the Sophocles' characters 'Black' voices remains one of the most hilarious, interesting, and nuanced works of ekphrasis (the creation of art based on a work of art) that I have ever witnessed. Later, when Hurricane Katrina happened, I remember the way you came into my room to hide from the world and put your head down on your desk. Then, at the end of your sophomore year, you were the first Black male to make the decision to take my AP English class. The conversations that we had about Aldous Huxley's *Brave New World* were incredible. Your analytical essays on the works of MLK, Malcolm X, Sojourner Truth, Susan Sontag, and Thoreau demonstrated your growth as a political thinker. I was so proud of you when you played the role of Barack

A DIFFERENT VISION

Obama in the mock election. You showed a lot of courage in getting up in front of the whole school to share your version of his political perspective.

When we went to the Black College Fair, I thought I saw a spark of interest in your eyes when you saw the presentation on Howard University. Throughout high school, I knew that you were facing some challenges at home. Like many students (and adults) in Portland, Oregon, I knew that you smoked marijuana. I didn't judge you, as the last three Presidents of the United States also admitted to ingesting it, as did some of the parents of wealthy white students who sat near you in class. When you got caught with the substance in your possession, I was devastated. I decided to show up to your expulsion hearing carrying every book that we ever read together. I made a plea for you to be allowed to remain in school. I think that you already knew what was going to happen, which is probably why you cried while I made my hopeful plea to the administration. They refused to allow you back on school premises. Despite your talents, you did not graduate from high school.

I was shocked to hear that you were going to prison. I am still shocked right now. You allowed me to see your brilliance. I cannot accept the reality that you will be locked up until 2021. I realize that the actions you committed, though you did not physically injure anyone, have consequences. But I have to reflect on the ways the school system treated you, often asked to leave classrooms based on a misunderstanding of your humor and general repression of your individuality. I have to consider the ways the system marginalized and set you up for defeat before you had the chance to thrive. I know that, as a man, you do accept full personal responsibility for your choices. I write this because

I remember how no parent representative was required to be present at the expulsion hearing. You had to go alone. I tried my best advocate for you, but I want you to know that in the future I will shout a little louder. Maybe this is my way of doing that. I hope you can hear me from behind the prison walls. I'll see you on the flipside. Stay strong.

Love,

Ms. Anglada Bartley

The Systemic Practice of Race-based Exclusion

After hearing a story like the one relayed above in the letter to my former student, it is easy to allow the mind to wander to other questions. Some might try to analyze the underlying problems with the goal of understanding what happened in the student's home to, ultimately, cause the prison sentence. However, among educators, the "social work" perspective can lead to a failure to look at our actions and an inability to recognize the failure of our system.

When I look at the student's personal life, I see parallels to my own. I lived with my single mother throughout most of high school. I smoked marijuana from time to time and sometimes carried it on my person; I trespassed; I even stole. These parallel actions never caught up with me, as I was able to hide behind the privilege of my skin color. No teacher suspected me. Since I was never suspected, I was never caught. No social worker ever used my family dynamics as an excuse to eject me from the learning environment. No one ever held a meeting, in the absence of my mother, where I was expelled from school. On top of experiencing systemic exclusion, students of color also endure humiliation at the hands of white social workers, teachers acting beyond their capacity, and administrators looking into their personal

lives to scrutinize the ways their family dynamic is causing their failure. Somehow, these same individuals rarely
practice such high-level scrutiny in regards to the system
they operate within. Nor do they examine the actions and
motives of the racist attitudes and practices of educators in
the school. This apathetic approach alienates families, places
students under the frightening microscope of white analysis,
and deepens feelings of hatred toward school. Examining
each student's individual situation, without evaluating the
role and presence of white supremacy and systemic exclusion in schools, will never help the system itself to emerge
from the practice of race-based exclusion.

The Failure of Discipline

What does this author mean when she says that *our system
is the problem*? Is she saying that *I* am the problem? As a
white North American teacher, I see how educators could
view these bold statements as criticisms or insults. Most
educators work tirelessly to sustain a system that is so poorly
funded that we sometimes have to subsidize it ourselves.
Each year, I pour hundreds of dollars into purchasing materials for the start of the year. Like countless teachers, I pour
my heart into my work, regularly searching for reservoirs of
emotional energy to meet the needs of my many students.
Likewise, parents and community members devote hours of
time and thousands of dollars in taxes to uphold this system,
while administrators search for ways to fix the problem
while dealing with the pressure of a litany of government
requirements, as well as the high-powered testing machines,
like Pearson. How dare a fellow teacher suggest that we,
as educators, community members, administrators, and
legislators have more work to do to fix our system?

If we don't recognize the failure of our system to promote students of color the way we do white students, then we, American educators and community members are participants in the demise of our system. More importantly, we are accepting paychecks (and, as taxpayers, signing checks) within an educational system that we know promotes suffering and social injustice based on race. It is disheartening to think that the work we have to do is even harder than the work we are already doing. It is demoralizing to realize that some of our good intentions, some of our begging and pleading, and some of the way we punish are part and parcel to institutionalized racism, but we can't stare the data in the face and turn away.

The United States Department of Education's Office for Civil Rights is conducting an ongoing, long-term investigation of Exclusionary Discipline and Race. A letter from the Office of Civil Rights to Administrators and Principals issued on January 8, 2014, reads:

> African-American students without disabilities are more than three times as likely as their white peers without disabilities to be expelled or suspended. Although African American students represent 15% of students in the CRDC, they make up 35% of students suspended once, 44% of those suspended more than once, and 36% of students expelled. Further, over 50% of students who were involved in school-related arrests or referred to law enforcement are Hispanic and African American.

The Office of Civil Rights explains the link between exclusionary discipline, drop-out rates, poverty, and imprisonment. Adding to that, the American Civil Liberties Union (ACLU) reports that, in California:

> In 2012-13, African-American students made up 6.3 percent of total enrollment, but 16.2 percent of suspensions. Latino students made up 52.7 percent of total enrollment, but 54.6 percent of suspensions. White students made up 25.5 percent of total enrollment, but 20.9 percent of suspensions.

In fact, in California, Law AB 420 limits the use of the catch-all category known as "willful defiance," which, according to ACLU, "includes minor disruption and accounts for 43% of suspensions issues to California students." Based on the presented data, 43% of suspended California students, constituted by an inordinate number of students of color, are excluded from school based on minor disruptions.

Exclusion from the learning environment as a form of punishment is harmful because students are often behind in their work when they return to class, which leads to widespread failure and lower graduation rates for Black and Latino students, nationally. This downward spiral, often starting from a minor misunderstanding created by a cultural crevasse, leads to the total demise of pedagogical trust, and can lead to imprisonment—the ultimate form of exclusion—rather than graduation and college attendance. The school-to-prison pipeline, well documented in Michelle Alexander's book *The New Jim Crow*, contends that the criminal justice system inordinately and historically imprisons people of color at far higher rates than whites. As educators, we must intentionally focus on the ways our school discipline systems begin this process of criminalization through behavior referral systems. Referrals may seem benign while writing one for a disruptive student, but they trigger the development of unacceptable statistics that demonstrate documented racism. The statistical data indicates the targeting of youth of color in U.S. public schools; we must accept responsibility and transform our system immediately.

We, teachers, do have a role in writing the millions of behavioral referrals that create these statistics. We document our institutionalized racism in a paper war against our students of color. Until now, our system has allowed us to use this archaic form of discipline to blame our students for their misbehavior with little self-reflection on our part. Likewise, school administrators regularly use disciplinary action against students of color and expel students of color at substantially higher rates than white students. The passage of AB 420 and the recent work of the Office of Civil Rights, under President Barack Obama, required educators and school administrators to consider how school discipline directly promotes racism and work towards change. The DeVos agenda to actively diminish the entire legacy of the Civil Rights Era is not a reason to lay down and stop fighting; it is the time to activate the energy of the resistance.

Beyond teachers and administrators, parents and community groups (like parent/teacher associations) also play a part in perpetuating racism in the educational sphere. These organizations are often sites where privileged white parents convene and devote countless hours to the school community. They regularly and naturally focus on upholding aspects of schools that serve their students, or the school as a whole (which is entrenched in institutional racism that they may not see)—rather than making civil rights the primary focus of their work.

How can parents, teachers, and administrators come together to change the system, so it benefits all students? This book will offer an examination of the multiple layers of institutionalized racism, while also providing solutions that require full participation from all three groups to move our schools forward. The following example, placing the focus on school discipline, offers a brief instance of methods we can employ to address exclusionary discipline.

I refuse to utilize my school's antiquated discipline system. Like some of my colleagues, I haven't written a referral in years. The absence of referrals doesn't mean I haven't got problems, but consciously I chose to never, ever use that antiquated system again. I decided that no matter how hard it was, I would find a way to solve my problems inside the classroom or with the help of the mental health professionals in my school. Acting alone to refuse to utilize the discipline referral system in your school district is one way to start challenging racism in your school. We must also band together as educators to demand change and reject the current disciplinary system. Rethinking Schools and the American Institute for Research (AIR) have published fascinating articles on the effects of exclusionary discipline. Subsequently, supportive forms of school discipline, including mediation and restorative justice programs, are under consideration in many school districts. The voices of teachers and community members are needed to demand their immediate implementation. Requesting system transformation by writing letters, showing up at board meetings, and refusing to utilize the current system are ways that we can make an impact right now. Administrators, too, must organize themselves and begin to resist the systems of oppression. See chapter seven for more on transforming administration.

Failure to See Racism vs. Denial

The institutionalized racism present in school disciplinary practices is prevalent and well-documented because educators and community members (sometimes unwittingly) participate in the implementation of such practices. Failure to see racism and denial are, sadly, always part of systematic oppression. If we could clearly see how we perpetuate racism, many would not participate. And many discontinue their teaching careers when they realize how firmly white supremacy is rooted in our educational system. Denial is different than failing to see racism. Failure to see racism is when a person cannot see the detrimental outcomes of their racist behavior. Denial is when a person is aware, to some degree, and chooses to proceed with the pretense that their actions are either justified or not causing the harm that it does cause.

Blame goes part and parcel with denial; to deny our culpability, we blame the system as a whole. Fellow educators often site large class sizes as the reason why they cannot deal with "difficult students." They are partially correct—underfunded schools are the macro-level culprit in the crusade against students of color. But in reality, we need well-funded schools *and* teachers and administrators who are willing to do the work required to dismantle the school culture of white supremacy that lingers like a cruel vestige of pre-civil rights America and colonialism. The illustration below shows a common pattern seen throughout U.S. High Schools.

Take a few minutes to explore in writing: *Can you observe a similar pattern in your place of work or school community? How would you alter this illustration and the descriptions to depict the cycle of school discipline in the school you work in?*

Typical Cycle of School Discipline

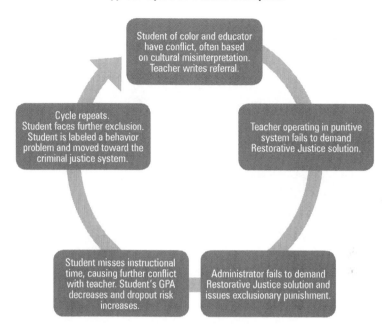

If we see this system of exclusionary discipline functioning in most U.S. schools, why don't we change it? Sadly, the system is protected by a shroud of denial. The illustration below shows a typical pattern through which school racism is protected and maintained.

Questions for Reflection:

Do you see this pattern occurring in your school community? How would you change the illustration to more accurately describe, precisely, what you see happening in your school environment?

Institutionalized Racism Protection Cycle

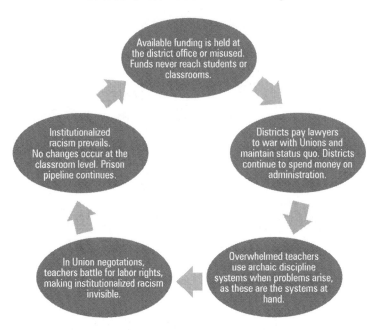

The perspectives included in this chapter are designed to shed light on how disciplinary models for youth perpetuate racism in schools, causing widespread system failure. This information is intended for sharing so that teachers, administrators, and community members can analyze how these dynamics operate in the schools that they serve or ask questions of the schools that their children attend. Since white educators failing to see racism is an essential ingredient in the functioning of systemic racism, we can dismantle it through seeing it, acknowledging it, and demanding change.

CHALLENGE:

Consider your own context—what does the flowchart for a positive system of student management look like? How do individual empowerment, family participation, and teacher and administrative accountability and self-reflection function in this new vision?

Patterns of Exclusion Beyond Discipline

Exclusionary discipline is just a gear in the system of educational inequity. Exclusion of students of color from advanced and college credit courses, whether intentional or not, stems from the racial bias present in school discipline systems. The prohibition the system places on students of color causes them to feel a lack of efficacy in their education, leading to higher rates of dropping out, living in poverty, and/or becoming fodder for the school-to-prison pipeline. The exclusion of students of color from such courses dates back to the development of agricultural colleges.

The first universities to serve Black people in the United States had to operate under the guise of only offering courses in agriculture or education (areas that did not threaten to create competition with whites in careers that earned higher wages or social status). Throughout the 1970s and 80s, this exclusionary pattern continued through urban centers with the implementation of technical and trade high schools in communities with high levels of poverty and high rates of students of color. The educational limits placed on marginalized students persists, nationally, as hundreds of thousands of schools systematically exclude students of color and students living in poverty from college-prep, AP, and college credit courses.

The exclusion of students of color from college-prep opportunities, like in the case of discipline, occurs at the teacher, counselor, and administrative levels. Educators and community members rarely scrutinize AP programs that are historically white. In fact, the majority of the high schools listed as the top 100 in the U.S., may practice exclusion of students of color in advanced level courses. Most reputable magazines that report on "top schools" do not use an equity informed lens to assess school ratings. In Portland, for example, the two high schools with the highest overall test scores are listed among the top four in the state, but in comparison to other schools in the district, both have far lower inclusion rates of students of color and students living in poverty in their AP programs. In other words, school assessment tools are designed to promote schools that are best for white students, but the same schools often fail, exclude, or reject their students of color.

By excluding students of color from advanced level courses, racism and white privilege in public education is rewarded, further punishing students of color. In contrast, white students who attend schools that are primarily white and wealthy gain college-prep capital by attending highly-rated schools with pristine school records, fewer disciplinary incidents, and excellent test scores. Likewise, affluent white students who take AP courses and "earn" high GPAs in schools where students of color do not have access to the same classes, ride into college on the backs of their excluded peers. It is time to ask ourselves, *is this the legacy that we wish to leave as educators, and as a nation?*

Inside schools, exclusion happens through a complex web of gatekeepers. At many schools, students have to sign paperwork and have their parent sign paperwork, to take an

AP course. Many schools require the previous year's teacher to sign off as well, indicating that student's level of preparation. Finally, the document reaches a school counselor, who may or may not place the student in the course. Imagine a student of color from a background where the parents did not attend college and did not speak English, or did not feel comfortable coming to the school to advocate for their child. Even if the student got the document signed by their parent, and the teacher did not agree or suggest the student for an AP course, the student may not gain access to the class. Usually, a much worse scenario takes place—often white supremacy in public education relies on institutional memory to thrive. For example, students of color frequently explain that they do not feel welcome in the AP courses because of the overwhelming amount of white students. AP teachers, counselors, and administrators at most schools are not doing the work of eradicating the barriers that exist for students of color to take AP and Dual Credit courses.

At the numerous schools I visited, the general assumption that students of color and students living in poverty are not able to do it and/or not prepared for AP courses festered. Teachers, counselors, and administrators commonly rationalize denying students of color and students living in poverty entrance to advanced classes by asserting that their parents do not possess a high-level of education. Some argue that their parent cannot support them with the work, and as such, the student, should not be promoted to more rigorous courses without the proper level of preparation, which they most likely will not receive. Doing so would be *leading them to inevitable failure* (if the student does not speak English at a level of proficiency required for the AP course the same arguments are used to justify their exclusion).

All of these rationales function on fallacious logic. The College Board statistics show that exposure to college-level curriculum both increases student investment in their education and makes the students more likely to graduate from college. Several studies report that students who take at least one AP course, even if they do not pass the exam at the end of the year, tend to graduate from college at far higher rates than those who have never taken an AP course. This data translates to multi-generational success, as we know that children with parents who have had at least some college are more likely to attend college. In light of this, as educators, we can take part in positively influencing countless generations of the same family by helping just one student be the first in their family to attend college. Better yet, we can help future generations of hundreds of families by extending the opportunity for higher education to as many students as possible.

"Not All Students Are Meant to Go to College"

Another rhetoric of denial commonly used to relegate students of color to lower-levels of education is the latent-racism-riddled concept that "not all students are meant to go to college."

Of course, it's true—maybe all people are not meant to go to college. But nationally, the data shrieks that the students who are "just not meant to go to college" are more likely to be African American, Latino, or Native American. Nine times out of ten, in my personal experience, this ideology is brought up as part of the debate on what to do about *the race problem* or *closing the achievement gap*. Picture this typical scene: A bunch of mostly white educators in a staff meeting or professional development seminar or school board meeting are trying to come up with a solution to *the achievement gap*. Somebody brings up the idea of technical and trade schools as a way to engage *unmotivated* students in *hands-on* education that will *prepare them for a career*. But when they say *unmotivated*, they mean the students of color who we are failing to serve. When they say *hands-on*, they mean un-intellectual work that requires training, but not necessarily higher-order thinking. When they say *prepare them for a career*, they mean give them skills that they can use in a trade, as white supremacy has already decided that these students are unable, and our system is unwilling, to prepare them to become doctors, lawyers, etc.

In the years to come, Justice Scalia's most famous remarks will likely be, "Most of the black scientists in this country do not come from the most advanced schools..." Scalia added that Black students do better in a "slower track." This frightening attitude is perpetuated every day by school systems that begin tracking Black, Latino, and Native American children out of higher-level mathematics courses in elementary and middle school. Documenting data from 2013–14, Emily DeRuy, in her article, "Where Calculus Class Isn't an Option," published in *The Atlantic*, writes:

> Despite the fact that Latino kids make up a quarter of all public-school students and black children comprised more than 15 percent of students that year just a third of high schools where at least three-fourths of students were black and Latino offered calculus. Yet 56 percent of high schools where black and Latino kids made up less than a quarter of the student body offered the course.

To reach the highest levels of AP mathematics, a student must take Algebra in 8th grade so they can complete Advanced Algebra in 9th grade, Geometry in 10th grade, Pre-Calculus in 11th grade, and AP Calculus AB during 12th grade. Some students go so far as to take Advanced Algebra before reaching high school so that they may enter the second year of Calculus, AP Calculus BC, by senior year. Patterns of discrimination demonstrate that very few African American, Latino, and American Indian students are academically prepared for this reality, let alone made aware of the consequences of taking lower-level courses. Consequently, white students have a higher likelihood of exposure to challenging mathematics opportunities. As such, white students are predestined for glowing high school transcripts that are extremely sought after by colleges and universities, especially those that offer profitable mathematics-related career tracks, like computer programming, engineering, accounting, and economics. By marginalizing Black, Latino, and Native American students from advanced mathematics opportunities, the system also denies them the chance to compete with white peers. Contrastingly, the system's institutionalized racism ushers white students into advanced courses. Scalia became a national example of the prevailing racist attitudes toward Black students, but who is indicting the system—which relegates students of color to lower-level classes starting in the early grades?

Whatever the rhetoric, the reality remains that our educational system is excluding students of color from taking the advanced coursework needed to prepare them for college. People who do not attend college are likely to remain in poverty. An article by Hope Yen, published in the Huffington Post, reports that young adults with just a high-school diploma earned only 62 percent of the typical salary of college graduates. Yen shares that this is the largest gap in earnings between high school and college grads in the past 48 years. Thus, when educators and community members say that not all students are meant to go to college, one must also infer that they are suggesting that not all people deserve to earn a viable income. White students have far higher college attendance and graduation rates than students of color, exposing the latent racism in our educational system.

In light of documented racist outcomes, the debate should not be about whether "all students should go to college" or not. Rather, we must shift the focus to eradicating barriers so that all students who desire the opportunity for higher education may proceed in that direction on equal footing. Those who get stuck in the semantics unintentionally (or perhaps subconsciously) hold us back from working to remove obstacles for students of color who wish to attend. Next time you hear educators or community members asserting that "not all people are meant for higher education," intently observe. Some will continue with an "economic argument" in which they state that society requires an unskilled underclass, essentially arguing that not all people are suited for a college education. This thought process is problematic because we must remove the barriers for Black and Brown students before we can properly assess who does and does not want to attend or have the intellectual capacity to attend. Otherwise, we perpetuate a caste system that inordinately throws Brown and Black children into that underclass of unskilled workers. Furthermore, we do so in a nation that has outsourced our "unskilled labor" and simultaneously created a profitable prison system to welcome those who are uneducated and unemployed. Sadly, this is not a dystopian vision of what could be; it is precisely how the system operates right now.

> ### Education is a Right: Students, Teachers, and Community Members Make Bill of Rights for Diversity
>
> Education is a human right. Growth and ingenuity are unalienable. Innumerable politicians, administrators, and school board members relentlessly uphold barriers to higher education. I have found that the best solution is to continue the work of clearing the path to higher education by removing obstacles in my school one by one, and by connecting with university-level educators and college recruiters who believe that all children should have the opportunity for higher education.
>
> Recently, a group of my former students who are now college graduates, Gates Millennium Scholars, or current college students, worked together with teachers and community leaders to create a Bill of Rights and Statement of Needs for Students of Color in AP and International Baccalaureate (IB) courses. We then gathered community support and proposed these changes to our school board and superintendent. We also sent the document to the Oregon State Board of Education, and the Office of Equity at both the district and state level. Take a look at this Bill of Rights and consider how you might amend it to eradicate gatekeeping in your community.

BILL OF RIGHTS
For Students of Color in AP and IB Courses

In recognition of existing civil rights legislation supporting each child's right to a free and public education; and in recognition of the existing deficit between the quality of

education provided to and the rates of high school graduation and college attendance for white students and students
of color, nationally and locally; with awareness of the facts
that colleges and universities are more likely to accept and
offer merit scholarships to students who engage in Advanced
Placement and International Baccalaureate courses; and
with the understanding that 82% of U.S. teachers are white,
and over 50% of students in public schools, nationally, are
students of color; and, in recognition that Portland Public
Schools struggles with an even greater gap between rates of
white teachers and students of color; and, in full acknowl-
edgement of the history of marginalization of students of
color in Advanced Placement and International Baccalaureate courses in Portland and nationally; and, in recognition
of the school-to-prison that so clearly discourages students
from both graduation and education, we, teacher Susan
Anglada Bartley, former AP students Lamarra Haynes (PSU
Graduate & Community Activist), Brook Thompson (Gates
Millennium Scholar & Yurok Tribe Member), Eyerusalem
Abebe (American University), Tori Cherisme (OSU Diversity
Scholar), Kaela Smith (PCC), Olivia Jones-Hall (Oberlin
College), Lu Imbriano (Wesleyan University), Alexis Phillips
(Gates Millennium Scholar) hereby present this Bill of Rights
and Statement of Needs in solidarity with the next generation
of students of color.

Bill of Rights for Students of Color in Advanced Placement and International Baccalaureate Courses:

- Students have the right to select the course they
  desire in order to gain exposure to material that will
  help them to succeed in the collegiate environment.

- No school employee should be entitled to discourage a student from participating in an AP or IB course.

- Students of color and students living in poverty must be fully informed about the opportunity for advanced coursework and encouraged to engage in such coursework.

- Students of color and students living in poverty have the right to choose AP or IB courses, and must not be prevented from doing so based on assumptions about inability or low expectations.

- Counselors must not remove students from AP or IB courses without involving three or more systems of support for students of color that are available in the school (for example, Culturally Specific Support Services, Tutoring, Special Education, only if applicable, and mentors).

- Counselors must be trained in culturally relevant strategies to help ensure specific support needs of students of color in AP and IB courses (Imposter Syndrome, isolation, etc.).

- The school Principal's signature must be required for removal of a student from an AP or IB course. We have too often seen, nationally and locally, students of color removed from AP or IB courses after having signed up. Centralizing the authority of removal of students will track removal as well as support provided, and ensure that students of color are not removed at inordinate rates.

Statement of Needs:

Teachers of AP and IB courses must be required to demonstrate the ways in which they are working to make their courses culturally relevant and accessible to all students.

Teachers of AP and IB courses must be required to certify that they understand the available supports and that they understand that all students have the right to take their chosen courses, as no student can be legally denied an opportunity in a public school environment.

- If a student struggles with absenteeism, school policy allows students to complete coursework up to a certain point in June. In some cases, home visits by social workers or support staff affiliated with Portland Public Schools (PPS) would be helpful in ensuring that students have the supports they need to face the challenging workload during the school year. These supports must be made available through the District; if they already exist, teachers must be made aware of exactly how to utilize these services.

- The District must invest a minimum of $15,000 at each high school and middle school to offer summer Bridge programs to help provide additional preparation for AP and IB courses. Students who do not take Algebra before entering high school have zero chance of reaching the highest level of AP/IB mathematics. Students of color have extremely low rates of participation in the highest level of AP/IB mathematics and science courses. We can remedy this by providing access to summer Bridge programs taught by certified teachers and with the support of partner agencies between 7th and 8th grades, 8th and 9th grades, and 9th and 10th grades.

- The District must waive the requirement to give all students a letter grade. Struggling students (of any background) should have the option to choose to take the course for a Pass or Fail or on a proficiency-based grading model, until mid-semester, in order to remain engaged in the course without damage to their GPA. While colleges will notice if a student chose to take the course for a Pass or Fail, they will also note that the student stayed in the course and continued to experience a higher level of preparation and exposure to the college-level material. Subsequently, counselors will have another option besides removing students from the course, and also reduce stress and anxiety for students taking AP or IB courses for the first time who may fear the consequences of a lower grade.

- Teachers must be made aware of the multiple supports that are available to help traditionally marginalized students in the AP/IB courses. Each teacher must be provided with a list of supports in the community and school that they may access when a student struggles.

- When a school doesn't have enough textbooks or materials, parents are often expected to backfill. This should not be the default option because not all students have parents who can pay for these items. Many AP/IB classes require the right calculator or laptop for reports, papers, and lab projects. Each high school must be supplied a minimum of $20,000 per year to cover the growing cost of AP/IB program supplies and textbooks.

- Each high school must be supported with funds to support AP/IB test fees for students living in poverty who cannot pay them. Currently, State support of this piece is deeply appreciated for AP. In some years, however, the State only pays part of the fee, still requiring students living in poverty to pay some amount. Schools must be able to easily access funds for students who cannot pay in an expedient way that will not cause delay. Delay is more likely to lead to the student not taking the test. Making $5000 available to each school for AP/IB testing fee scholarships for students on Free and Reduced (F&R) Lunch as well as students who are on the poverty line (though they may not be documented as F&R) will remove barriers.

- District partners must work toward supporting students of color in AP and IB courses, and prepare themselves with knowledge and training about AP and IB curriculum so that they may best support students taking the courses.

- Parents must be notified of the existence of AP and IB programs, summer Bridge programs, as well as the courses that students must engage in during 7th and 8th grade in order to prepare for higher-level courses. This information must be available in all languages that are spoken in the school environment.

- Schools with higher percentages of students of color and students living in poverty must be offered Advanced Academic Curricular options at the same rate as students in schools with higher percentages of white students and students of privileged socio-economic status. Schools with higher socio-economic levels and higher percentages of white students must be offered Career and Technical Education at the same rate as schools with higher numbers of students of color and students living in poverty.

After writing the Bill of Rights with the aid of former students, we presented it to a series of fellow teachers and national education researchers to gather support. We then presented the document to the PPS School Board and superintendent. To keep the pressure on them to adopt this bill, I sought support from other educators, legislators, and even from the hip-hop community. We gained the backing of Olympic gold medalist and founder of Classroom Champions, Steve Mesler, as well as multi-platinum rapper Scarface. The local news media followed the story, as did state Senators Jeff Merkley and Ron Wyden. We emailed the superintendent and the School Board with a few new supporters each week to demonstrate an inimitable solidarity. Gaining the support of activists from Don't Shoot Portland, Black Lives Matter Portland, and the League of Women Voters was crucial to our success. Ultimately, the Bill was accepted with a unanimous vote from the Portland School Board and a public letter of support from our superintendent. The next step will be holding them accountable to their commitment.

Questions for Reflection: Teachers, Community Members, Parents, and Administrators:

1. Do inequities exist in my district regarding AP and IB programs? What percentage of students of color are engaged in these courses?
2. Does gatekeeping begin during 6th or 7th grade for students of color, causing them to be unprepared to take higher-level courses in high school?
3. What summer Bridge opportunities exist (not remediation opportunities, but chances to take higher-level courses during the summer to remedy existing barriers)? How could I take part in building this type of program, providing support as a parent or parent-teacher-student association (PTSA) member, or securing funds and dedicating my focus as an administrator?
4. How are students made aware of opportunities for advanced coursework? Is the information available in multiple languages?
5. What are the attitudes of teachers in my school regarding the inclusion of students of color in AP/IB courses? Is there a deficit model of thinking (one in which students of color are viewed as incapable or bound for failure), or an attitude of the right to exposure? Right to exposure means: educators have the attitude that all students are welcome to engage in the coursework of their choice, and that students will rise to the expectations if given the support they need.

The Untracked AP Movement is a teacher and student-led movement to eradicate barriers to AP courses. Incredible educators, like Joan Cone out of Los Angeles, and others throughout the United States have revolutionized their school environments to rid their schools of barriers for students of color and students living in poverty who wish to take AP courses and attend college. These barriers manifest in the form of practice, personnel, school culture and institutional memory, or the dominant ideology of the teaching community.

There are undoubtedly documented inequities, nationally, in the numbers of students of color who enroll in AP and IB courses versus the number of white students. However, there is still a debate among education activists regarding the best way to approach this problem. Some argue that the College Board, because it is part of the testocracy that creates the ugly paradigm by which we measure student success through the value of assessments that are inherently in favor of white supremacy, must be taken down entirely. I agree, yet I also accept the reality that colleges and universities rely on these institutions when considering students for admission. The measuring of young people by one expensive yardstick for each subject is a measurement of the degree to which we require conformity to Euro-Americentric values. To counter this, colleges and universities must revolutionize admissions processes. Until then, we must continue to pressure the College Board and AP and IB corporations to address inequity in their corporate model. The Advanced Placement Board, though not an organization I can entirely defend, has made moves toward diversifying their tests in AP English Literature, AP English Language, and AP Art History. The open questions on the 2015 AP English Literature exam, for example, used authors of color for all examples and added a final question on a social justice oriented theme. Changes in these areas are not enough; the entire curriculum and testing systems must be reviewed by scholars of color to radically alter the systems as a whole. Considerable work will be necessary to dismantle bias in the AP and IB testing methods; the AP community is in fact engaged in this process, with leaders of color at the helm in several vital areas. As usual, the degree to which equity-focused educators can make impactful decisions in a corporate setting correlates with the degree of racism in society at large. We cannot expect perfection from them until we demand full inclusion (and even then, we will have to fight against bias in their corporate environment). The deeper problem continues at the school level, where old ideas about who can excel prevail, perpetuating systemic marginalization.

To see how we implemented an inclusive AP program at Franklin High School in Portland, Oregon, see the Appendix.

2

Self-Knowledge Through Story

Corporate interests dominate public education, acting as test-score obsessed succubi on students, schools, and communities. With this corporate drain, the heart of what it means to be a great teacher is lost. Meanwhile, young people face a more savage capitalism than ever before, corporate interests vibrating in their pockets, the chatter of celebrity is a new silence. To engage the new generation, we must radically alter the entire focus of our system to centralize the human element. We must fight for our students by helping them contextualize their existence in this moment on the planet. By teaching students to understand their power, as well as the obstacles that they face based on race, gender, economics, and sexuality, we can prepare them to live in this world. Through empowering them to embrace new media to retell their stories and connect with others, we can move against the overwhelming corporate leviathan that we all carry. As educators, parents, and community leaders, we can start by telling our stories. In this media-obsessed historical moment, standing in our vulnerability, exposing our flaws, and sharing our life lessons is among the most radical actions that we can take as adults.

I don't tell my story all at once—it comes out as we study different poems throughout the year, it comes out while I am working with a student on their college essay, it comes out when the moment calls for it—knowing when is another magical part of the craft that comes only through learning to listen for what students need to hear.

My mother came from a family of addicts, and in the early 1980s, my Uncle Brian was simultaneously at the height of his heroin addiction and my favorite person alive. He was a hilarious, talented, charismatic, red-headed storyteller who I deeply loved. During the Buffalo winter, we had to lock him out of the house because he couldn't help but steal to feed his addiction. I remember the way my breath fogged up the front window as I watched him shiver on the pavement outside—he was allowed to stay there waiting in front of the house because he had nowhere else to go, but we couldn't let him in.

Not too long after my parents' divorce in the late eighties, my grandmother, who lived with my mother, brother, and I, grew sick with lung and eye cancer. Her eye was removed, and she wore a patch. Sadly, she continued to smoke cigarettes—smoke would billow out of the hole where her eye once was, but all I saw was the reflection of my broken heart when she smiled lovingly towards me. Throughout her illness, my Uncle Brian experienced a major transformation--he enrolled in a methadone clinic and began to lead a slightly more stable life (we could trust that he wouldn't steal from us and he sometimes came over to mow the lawn). As part of his healing process, he took my grandmother to her doctor's appointments, bathed her, and helped her through the process of dying.

As I entered adolescence, my uncle, still using methadone and leading a comparatively stable life to his previous
life as a con-artist and criminal, took up residence, rent-
free, in an unrentable property located in an impoverished
part of Buffalo that belonged to a friend of my mother. My
uncle's residency was, in a way, the owner's way of preventing the house from becoming a full-fledged crack house. My
uncle used extension cords to run space heaters throughout
the property and put up giant sheets of plastic to keep in
the heat. The front door had five locks as well as a four by
four that acted as a barricade. Prostitutes and crack addicts
convened in the abandoned lot next door.

Throughout the early 90s, my uncle continued to import
large amounts of marijuana into this house. He also grew
his own designer strains in a secret room in the back of the
house. While his criminality continued, so did his compassion. He noticed a young Black man looking lost at the
corner store, found out that he was homeless and down and
out in Buffalo from the South Bronx. My uncle took him
in, and also invited the man's son and mother (who had
AIDS and had recently been released from prison) to live
at the residence. This man became like a son to my uncle,
but also a great protector. When a team of armed robbers
busted into the house, this young man jumped out when
they pointed the assault rifle my uncle's face and pushed
the gun away, just in time for the bullet to shoot through
the floor. The assailants butted the young man's face with
the end of the gun before leaving, breaking his nose. As
a child, I gained a hardcore understanding of loyalty and
sacrifice at a young age.

I visited my uncle weekly at this decrepit house; inside,
I always found him sitting in the same chair, smoking ciga-

rettes or marijuana, or breaking up bricks of marijuana or playing his guitar. The blue of the television screen always shown through the plastic sheets from the outside of the house. No matter what time of day or night, my uncle was available to tell stories. His stories ranged in subject matter, including his experience hitchhiking to and living in San Francisco when he was fifteen years old, his experience watching his older brothers become addicted to heroin in the 1960s, the drug house in Detroit being raided, the war on the poor, the war on Black people in urban centers, the war on the environment, the history of rock & roll, blues, and the Hippie Movement, Henry David Thoreau's *Walden* and the poetic work of Walt Whitman, the supremacy of animals over humanity, the heroic rise and fall of Jimi Hendrix and Janis Joplin, the failure of the Reagan administration's economic policy and the harm it did to the mentally ill and the poor, the items he currently had in the pawn shop and what he planned to do to get them out, and the poor choices he had made in his life that I must never make. Throughout his fascinating lectures, he often punctuated his points with electric or acoustic guitar solos, or with long drags from a joint.

Learning from my uncle was absolutely part of my adolescent rebellion. He was an outstanding lecturer, a man in possession of a tremendous intellectual gift and the gift for storytelling that was passed down on the Irish side of the family. At the same time, he was a tortured soul, suffering from debilitating depression. I took some great lessons from this man. He clarified the path of death and destruction for me and pushed me toward a healthier path, both as an example and through the words he spoke to me. He also impressed me with a deep integrity—while he was living in abhorrent conditions, had no social status to speak of (other than a bit of a name as a marijuana importer), he never took one action that was against the values that he proclaimed. He was a stubborn, brilliant, radical individual who chose a life on the fringe of society—a depressed, addicted, urban Thoreau without all of the privileged relationships or a cool pond. Through knowing him, I gained several crucial insights for my work as a teacher. *Young people are looking for excellent storytellers and wish to be exposed to truth, even if it is ugly. Young people are fascinated by individuals who exist outside of the norms (they personally need to fit in, but long for role models who have the courage to be different).* And the most valuable lesson—*young people who I face in the classroom may be facing a complex array of difficulties that are totally invisible on the surface.* Compassion for the existence of these challenges, even if I cannot see them, is at the core of my work.

To dismantle and transform the "isms" of the system, we must willingly examine our personal relationships to race, class, gender, sexuality, and ability. This statement includes all people. Examination of the ways we have been silenced or silenced others, whether due to growing up in a racist environment or growing up in fear of racist whites, is required for us to move forward with courage. To transform the system, we must possess a profound sense of courage that we can only achieve through authentic self-knowledge. For this reason, this chapter offers a place to pause and intentionally engage in this lifelong process of combined self and social inquiry. This exploration is not only required for social transformation; it is also the cornerstone of excellent teaching and honest activism and community work. We received a key concept from Freire. We must shift our educational dynamic so that it centers equality in the relationship between student and teacher and the empowerment of students by the teacher. We must carry with us the incredibly humble, omnipresent consciousness that without the student *there is no teacher.* Anti-racist teaching must begin with the refusal to stand separate from the students at the front of the classroom. We must move the nexus of student and teacher consciousness to the heart center, building relationships through truth-telling. Active listening, on the part of the teacher, must replace lecturing; the role of a teacher must include the requirement to help students understand social reality and their place in it. We can only accomplish the level of self-knowledge required to help others understand their potential and obstacles within social reality by pausing long enough to understand our positionality in that reality, which includes self-analysis based on race, class, gender, and sexuality. The best I can do to guide you in this process is to offer you parts of my own story, as well as some great questions and resources for getting started on this work.

A Revolution of Relationships

The best teachers bring an awareness of the reality of human suffering into every aspect of their work. We don't solely teach about suffering, but we are invariably aware of the emotional reality present in our classroom and, as much as possible, the struggles that our students face. We must not look for ways to silence students; instead, we must look for ways to help them gain a resounding knowledge of the historical legacy of oppression that their ancestors survived so that they might exist in this moment. The more aware you are of the pain caused by racism, poverty, discrimination, marginalization due to gender, sexuality, mental illness, addiction, or different learning style, the more successful you can be at understanding, and genuinely showing compassion for your students. *The experience of acceptance that students feel in your presence will lay the foundation for openness to the content material that you are trying to deliver.* You will find greater ease in relaying information to your students when they experience you as a compassionate adult who knows their story and sincerely believes in them.

Young people are looking for opportunities to hear or view healing stories that help them to navigate their lives. Truthful storytelling is the best classroom management technique on the planet, while forced learning that lacks context will cause students to tune out and seek a more vibrant education from the world inside their pocket. In my own experience, young people have a natural capacity to see the hidden pain in adults. They are naturally looking for wise adult role models from whom they can learn how to proceed through life with strength. They are looking for people who seem successful on a soulful level, not necessarily because they are a doctor, lawyer, or a wealthy banker, but because they have learned how to live and find happiness, despite hardship. Students have sharp bullshit detectors. They are also aware that adults with hidden, unresolved pain can be hurtful towards them, as many have experienced this in their home environments.

There is magic in having a story to tell; young people are looking for healing stories. Their yearning is why so many hip-hop artists who are now approaching 40 or 50 years old retain their respect with the younger generation—their stories of survival against the odds still resonate. When students tune out in high school classes, they often look to videos that convey humor, wisdom, and life lessons that they connect with. The problem is never that young people don't want to learn; it is that they see through the thin, soulless veil of bogus, corporatized education. When you have an engaging story, even if you are white, you can share that story and students will listen. Likewise, Black, Latino, Native American, and Asian educators can relate to a broader range of students by revealing more of their true selves. Studies show that students of color gain more from hearing the stories of people of color who have endured challenges similar to those that they face (which is why part of the system's transformation will require the inclusion of teachers of color at numbers proportionate to the population of students being served). But, they also learn from educators of other races, including white educators if these educators are willing to commit to relating outside of the teacher-as-tyrant model.

How do you weave story-telling into a math class? You greet each student with simple questions every day that helps them to reflect on their emotional state, their overall goals, and their goals for the class itself. And you save a little bit of your magic wisdom for the end of class, love. They'll wait. Do your stories all have to relate to hardship? Not necessarily. You can share about your battle to learn guitar, your trip to Canada when you were 19, your remarkable journey to make the basketball team. Each of us has not just one story, but thousands. To revolutionize teaching, we must all view ourselves as mentors, but also as subjects of our students. *We must remember that each and every student may also provide valuable lessons for us—both lessons in teaching and in navigating life itself;* we must find the stories that inspire our students to be excited about life's possibilities; we must also share about the places where we failed and picked ourselves back up.

You can start to compile your stories by listing out your life's greatest lessons. Then work on writing out your eight best stories of fascination, and your five stories about challenges that you faced. Your willingness to share these stories with students, five minutes at a time, will transform the way that they view you and create space for relationships—and a sense of love and respect—that is an absolute gift every day.

Viewing myself as a mentor and story-teller for my students, as well as a transmitter of skills and knowledge, and continually honing my mentoring and storytelling skills is the single most important aspect of my craft as an educator. A great story has a universal quality, the ability to attract the attention of children of every nation. As the landscape of public education continues to shift, stories with global relevance must become the cornerstone of our work. For, when you share your willingness to expose your inner caverns of hardship, you will find that you have created a space for your students to do the same. Get ready for some moments of extraordinary love, listening, courage, tears, and the success that comes when we, through community, move past what holds us back.

Along with actively listening to others and exploring how racism affects students in our school environments, it is essential to understand your most intimate struggles; you have to go through the woods to get to the village. Looking into the ways you or members of your family have suffered, and doing the work of healing, will equip you as a leader who can bring others through life's dark passages. Think of the exceptional teachers you have had in your life, in or outside of an institution—they were healers who helped you to understand, accept, and love yourself. They were saints (or at least friendly souls) who marched with you, led you when you were lost, and gave you information to empower you through trying and dark times so you could continue walking toward the light.

Admirable teachers don't just have a set of strategies that they learned in a workbook or a graduate class. Admirable teachers have a deep soul power won from hard-earned life lessons that have crystallized into gems of wisdom that they willingly share with those who show them loyalty and trust. Workbooks and graduate programs can help you to become more skilled and organized; they can help you to diversify your methods. To be incredible, excellent and well-practiced methods, skills, and routines are essential—but wisdom, soul power, courage, faith, and compassion will also be required. To get these, we have to face ourselves.

For me, facing these dark corners achieved a grounded self-knowledge that better equips me to deal with a variety of students and situations. For me, this process involved looking back at my life, in terms of race, gender, and socio-economic status, and in terms of examining my pain, and working to heal it, so that I could be a better resource for others. I share the following example, modeling my experience, to clarify the kind of work required. I also share in case anyone reading might know, from reading it, that they are not alone. Finally, I want to express a nuance. The purpose of sharing one's story is not to show that we, as adults, exceeded the level of suffering experienced by diverse young people, *it is to connect by having experienced challenges and navigating through them.* Students will notice if we try to demonstrate a pretentious heroism; they are told all too often to toughen up and deal with their circumstances. They will appreciate honesty and adults who have a bit of wisdom to share. Sharing wisdom is different from sharing advice. Young people shut their ears when they know that advice is coming; but they gather around when an adult has wise reflections to offer, based on their personal experience. During my college career at New York University, I focused a great deal on finding ways to *tell my story*, both about my uncle and about other parts of my life. I only half realized that I was a young college kid on scholarship and that my story had just barely begun. When I look back at my writing now, I see that I was going through a healing process, trying to integrate a set of complex experiences to find new ground to walk forward on. It took me about fifteen years to understand that my story wasn't the significant part, but *the lessons that emerged from my story are essential gems of truth that guide my life's path.* I learned crucial lessons from my relationship with my uncle, and there many other parts of my life that taught me valuable lessons too:

While growing up, all of my mother's brothers were heroin addicts; the path to death and destruction was crystal clear—*I was given an incredible life lesson in what not to do.* I also learned a magnificent lesson about love—*love pervades beyond the walls of halfway houses, crack houses, prisons, untenable, borrowed, rent-free homes; love can be a powerful force between glass windowpanes or thousands of miles.*

My mother never attended college and worked 80 hours per week to establish a business in an abandoned building to help me pay for college. *I learned about the power of persistence, the belief in self, female power, the right to creativity despite circumstances, and the power of hard work.*

I became tangled up in the streets and had relationships with men who harmed me when I was looking for love. *I learned, very clearly, the value of my femininity and my sexuality; once I became self-possessed, not possessed by others or a sexist culture, I grew immensely in confidence.* I saw some of my friends from the hip-hop community either go to prison, pass away, or suffer in low-level jobs; *I learned, through people I loved and admired, about the power and privilege of whiteness. My work as a teacher continues to be informed by the understandings I gained about white supremacy and marginalization through living in Buffalo and studying with outstanding professors at NYU.*

My bright, intellectual father left our home when I was eight. He was my protector, and he was gone from my everyday life (though I visited him once per week for most of high school and he persistently showed me he loved me). *I learned how to stand up, choose sanity, and keep on living despite losing everything. I also learned how to escape, break free, and lead a new life from watching the choices that he made.*

From all of these truths, I find my motivation—to help young people see the ways hardships can prepare them for greatness (or at least success), and to help them understand how race, class, gender, and sexuality may impact, but not block, their path.

By working with students of color and understanding the legacy of racism in the United States, I see that though my story has elements of hardship, I did not experience *this while also experiencing systemic and institutionalized racism on a daily basis.* When I faced difficulties, I still held the privileges of whiteness. A vast set of privileges that include being more likely to be called on in class and encouraged and promoted into higher-level courses, the assumption of intelligence, generally learning from educators who looked like me, and earning diversity-based affirmative action scholarships to help fund my education due to being a white female. No one ever caught me for the hundreds of infractions that repeatedly sent young people of color to prison. I could smile and lie at the same time; rarely, if ever, did anyone doubt my intentions. Police officers have even helped me to break the law; for example, when driving without my license in Portland, Oregon in 2003, I was graciously sent on my way on the very same street where Portland Police officers shot and killed a Black woman, Kendra James, while she reached for her seatbelt so she could produce her license, which she did indeed have with her. This list does not even scratch the surface of the reality of racism in the United States. I will never know the exact nature or degree of privilege that I walk through life with each day; perhaps that is the highest privilege of all.

Students appreciate hearing that I am an individual who has a story. They like to relate to a person—not to a cardboard cut-out who has mastered the art of feigning control. In working with students of color, I have noticed that hearing bits of my story can make me seem like a real, multi-dimensional person—and they often take the tidbits that I offer as invitations to share bits of their own story. The key for both teacher and student is taking the time to understand our stories, and going a step beyond by *distilling the truth*, and figuring out how to use the wisdom learned from our stories as a vehicle to progress towards our dreams. As educators, we can use the relationship built through our stories to help students gain self-perspective, find the strength in their struggles, and embrace their power in spite of challenges.

Take some time to write out your story. Writing your story will not be a short assignment. You may need several journals. You may need a counselor or a support group. I needed all of the above. I also had the privlege to separate myself from reality for a month and study yoga and meditation (movement and cultural appropriation will be discussed in Chapter Six). While I couldn't stay out there, I realized, through looking intensely within myself, that I am eternally connected to an immense source of energy and love that is with me to this day.

My Connection Story Working Questions:

1. What are the greatest challenges that I have faced in my life?
2. Looking at the list I've made, how does membership to a historically oppressed racial or ethnic group or white privilege relate to my narrative?
3. How did I overcome these challenges? What people or resources did I access to navigate these challenges? What inner resources did I use to overcome these challenges? What privileges did I have to help me to make it through these challenges?
4. How do class, gender, and sexuality relate to my story? After examining these, take another look at race and white privilege. What advantages did I have or obstacles did I uniquely face, regarding race and/or white privilege, in navigating obstacles based on class, gender, or sexuality?

Distilling: the Deeper Soft Skill

5. What individuals in my life most inspired me? What earnest lessons did they teach me that I would like to share with students? If there was one skill (courage, persistence, passion, etc.) that this story could help students to understand, what would that be?
6. How can I use this story to teach the skill while allowing students to speak back to me about the meaning of this skill *through sharing their own example and story*?

If I can invite in the stories of my students by creating a comfortable classroom community for vulnerability, I can practice culturally relevant teaching authentically—*by allowing students themselves to share knowledge and teach one another about what they know about navigating life itself*. In a diverse environment, their stories will inherently involve lessons related to race, class, power, gender, sexuality, and privilege. My job as a teacher is to hold the space for this powerful story-telling to take place. This can be a community project that occurs over time—so that one student shares per day or every few days for the first two months. It can happen in ten to twenty minutes at the end of class; it can also happen in small groups; or, it can happen in private conversations with every student if you are not ready for the experience of an open floor. Regardless of how it happens, you will have increased success in teaching your subject matter when you invite the whole student into the classroom and show that you value their life stories and life lessons as much or more than Shakespeare's Sonnets or π.

We cannot emerge, as a society, from our racist past without wholly shifting the ways in which we communicate with one another as human beings. I would like to believe that we can simply transform our entire system through storytelling, but we must dive into the depths, understanding how racism operates in the society, school, and classroom. The United States currently has more people imprisoned than any other country on earth. Black, Latino, and Native American people disproportionately fill our prisons. We can now, unquestionably, correlate the experiences of Black, Latino, and Native American youth in school environments to the patterns of imprisonment. The upcoming chapters will invite the reader to awaken to the ways that accepted strategies for behavior management uphold a system of racist exclusion.

Parents, Community Members, and Teachers Coming Together through Story:

By helping a student contextualize their lives and build goals, they begin to understand the path to success. Even more, they start showing a willingness to accept help. Young people whose parents did not attend college do often need additional help to understand the college application process and to refine their personal statements for admission and scholarship applications. In the past five years, seven of my students received the prestigious Gates Millennium Scholarship, and hundreds of other students won private scholarships through foundations or colleges. Storytelling and mentoring from caring adults played an immeasurable role in supporting these students, all of whom were willing to navigate their inner worlds to tell their incredible stories about how they navigated their life circumstances to succeed.

At Franklin High School in Portland, Oregon, parents, teachers, and community members come together once per year to offer a college essay writing project. After reading an email from the Executive Director of Writers in the Schools, Mary Rechner, in which she explored the development of a college essay writing project, I worked with her to develop a sturdy college-essay writing workshop to support students who were working on their college essays. The project is open to all 12th-grade students (and 11th graders if there is room on the roster), the objective is to ensure support for students who may not have a parent at home who can read and assist with their college essays.

In preparation for the event, Mary and her assistant Mel Wells solicited a superb team of volunteers. Some were retired teachers or school counselors, others writers from the community, some parents from our school community. Over time, Mel and Mary linked up with business and community organizations that helped to provide more mentors of color, so that we could, as much as possible, connect students with adults who made it past many of the same types of obstacles that the students face themselves as people of color. We made sure that all adults passed a background check, and I created a training to share my best tips on the college essay, as well as tips for being around teenagers. After all the parents received preparation, we set an after-school date, recruited students, ordered pizza for the students since they were coming after school, and provided excellent mentoring to now hundreds of students over a period of four years. In addition to the need for college essay mentors, there is a great need for connection to healthy, stable adults among many children in our school environments. Does your high school currently provide an opportunity for mentors to work with young people who need additional help to understand the path to college, navigate their classes, or who merely want to connect with a healthy, sane adult? If you are a teacher, do you continue to view yourself as a mentor as well as a transmitter of information? One golden role that I have found to be true when working with students of color is that many need to experience my humanity and learn to see me as a real person before they are willing to trust and accept me as their teacher. Connection is essential.

PART II

Beyond Inclusion - Relationships to Build Pedagogical Trust and Equity

I n envisioning a new model for education that will transform the system from within, we must stop using *control* to order our classrooms and instead use a *trust*. In examining the history of education in the United States, it is evident how and why the operable system is based on control. Here is, for me, a shocker—according to the Center for Effective Discipline, nineteen states still allow corporal punishment in schools. Research shows that corporal punishment is less common than it once was, but it is not illegal in *every* state. My point is that we, as a nation, haven't moved far from a style of pedagogy based on physical force.

Even though I live in a state that does not allow the subjugation of young people to corporal punishment, I see vestiges of it every day. It seems that states that no longer allow corporal punishment have just shifted to using other forms of humiliation to require students to submit to learning. While the use of humiliation to control human beings is detrimental to all, evidence shows that Black, Latino, and Native American children are disciplined far more than their white peers. If existing records demonstrate this inequity, how many instances of unrecorded humiliation occur in classrooms daily? It's time to go in an entirely new direction—through the replacement of classroom management (classroom control) with the implementation of pedagogical trust. When our students trust us, they believe that what we have to teach them is valuable.

To establish pedagogical trust, we must build stronger bridges to the communities that we serve. We must build a system that strengthens the relationship between the teacher and the families they serve. Both to bolster trusting relationships between the teacher and her community, but also to provide a structure of support for the value of education itself. Educators must also be willing to re-examine entire curriculums to eradicate lessons and activities that require the expectation of power and control and involve pedagogical tactics based on humiliation. Through this revolutionary process, we must find ways to remain healthy, heart-centered, and focused on what matters-centering our educational system on values that support respect for all human life and the natural environment.

Teacher Questions for Reflection:

Please take some time to write about the people you wholeheartedly trust. The questions that I offer here are not facetious. They are
necessary to answer because we all come up in a society where
using violence to control children is the norm.
1. What does trust mean to you?
2. When you think about the people you trust, what is the foundation of that trust?
3. Does violence play a role in your reasons for trusting others?
Do you see a relationship between non-violence and trust?
4. What is the relationship between trust and control? Do you
agree that real trust means that one does not need to control
another?
5. How could you trust your students more and control them less?
6. What would you need to change about your teaching to imbue
your style with more trust and less control?
7. What do you need to do to transform control to trust in your
teaching?

After you've journaled your thoughts on these questions, the following chapters will help you examine them
further and provide you with practical tools for instilling
your classroom with pedagogical trust.

In addition to removing humiliation tactics from our
system, Chapter 3 and Chapter 4 offer opportunities to
reflect on the impacts of big data on curriculum design,
and suggestions for how educators and administrators
can better understand students, as making students feel
seen and understood can transform our methods and
practices. Finally, the work of transformed classrooms,
curriculum, and communities requires networks of allies

who support one another. Chapter 5 shares strategies for developing an effective group of change-makers at your school.

3

Dismantling the Culture of Humiliation

"Will Susie Bartley please come down to the Principal's Office?"

I shivered with fear as I heard my name called out over the loudspeaker for the whole school to hear. I didn't want to get up from my desk in 9th grade English, for I knew the reason for the public humiliation—my white jean shorts were too short to meet school standards. That was why I had put them on in the morning. I was wearing them for two reasons—to attract boys and be the coolest and most rebellious girl in my class.

I stood up and left the room, walking down the stairs from the third floor to the first, wrestling with deep feelings of fear and humiliation. But by the time I got to the first floor, white privilege had already swept in to save me—my older brother, who was at the time one of the top performing white male seniors and a National Merit Scholarship qualifier, had rushed down to talk to the principal before I could get there. He promised I would never wear those shorts again, saving my ass from a much harsher consequence than public humiliation on the loudspeaker.

I share this story to ask you to consider the ways educators used humiliation against you as a child in public or private education. While corporal punishment is no longer legal in most states, a culture of overt and subtle humiliation continues to govern the methodology and ideological foundation of discipline at both the classroom and larger school level.

> **Teacher, Parent, and Administrator Questions for Reflection:**
>
> Take some time to think through, or better yet *feel through*, episodes in which mild or severe humiliation was used to control you in your own educational experience:
> 1. What happened? Where were you?
> 2. Was the element of surprise used against you? Was sarcasm part of the teacher's "classroom management" toolkit?
>
> Take some time and write about the ways in which you were humiliated. If humiliation was never used against you:
> 3. Did you witness another student being humiliated? Describe the feelings you had while watching that.
> 4. Do you see how the humiliation of another student could contribute to your need to conform and fit in so that you would avoid the same fate?

The Humiliating Truth

Now let's expand the discussion. National statistics from Dignity in Schools show that African American students are at least 3.5 times more likely to be expelled than their white peers. The majority of these expulsions resulted from, "minor misbehavior," including "disruptive behavior, "or "insubordination." The NEA (National Education Association) reports that Black, Hispanic, and Native American students are suspended at twice the rate of white students.

These statistics do not begin to acknowledge the micro-aggressions and subtle but painful forms of humiliation that attempt to control students inside of classroom environments on a daily basis. The sad truth is that educational discipline in our country supports institutionalized racism, which, at its roots, begins with daily embarrassment and degradation.

We can start extracting the culture of humiliation, by removing the subtle student domination techniques that educators use in classrooms daily. I want it to be clear that eradicating humiliation from my "classroom management" toolkit is something that I, too, must constantly work toward. Teaching a large group of students without using humiliation, sarcasm, or other domination techniques requires meaningful reflection, inventiveness, creativity, and lots of role reversal and compassion.

Let me provide examples of how a culture of humiliation can lead to damaging relationships between educators (who, as previously stated, are 82% white in the United States) and students of color. Imagine an everyday scenario in which a teacher reprimands a student for having their cell phone out. With a classroom of 30 students, many educators deal with this situation by calling out the student in front of the whole class, reprimanding the student and asking them to put it away.

We already know that Black and Brown students are more likely to face this type of reprimand than white students; the students themselves are aware of this constant bias because it relentlessly happens to them. This reality of being called out negatively is repeated throughout their educational experience, which creates resentment. The educator may be reacting to a real (perceived) problem, however, calling out the student, whether with a harsh voice or a gentle one, in front of the whole class is the starting point for humiliation. It is as if the teacher is saying: if you don't put that phone away (or you don't stop talking in class, or you don't sit down), I am going to do or say something much worse in front of everyone. This dynamic is repeated every day, multiple times per day, by teachers who are both overburdened by large class sizes and who have few skills, other than those based in public humiliation, to relate to their classes.

Numerous theories attempt to explain why students of color are disciplined at higher rates. Some suggest that students of color harbor anti-authoritarian feelings due to years of being reprimanded in the system and therefore willingly push boundaries. Some suggest that students of color, who are also more likely to live in poverty, are more likely to act out in class due to lack of proper parenting. I wholeheartedly disagree with these theories. Many Black parents, for example, regularly speak with their children about the reality of dealing with white police and surviving within the reality of institutionalized racism in schools and society at large, yet this ignorant argument about family values persists. Educators who accept and operate under the assumption that parents of color or social factors out-side of school are to blame for the gratuitous exclusion of African American, students of Latin American heritage, and Native American students fail to take responsibility for the crime of institutionalized racism, and thereby promote it. Both theories, ultimately, excuse teachers and administra-tors from changing the racist systems of discipline that we use in our classrooms and schools. From my observation, humiliation, and exclusion of students of color stem from the unethical manner in which classroom and school management are executed in U.S. public schools. In my own experience, educators can remedy harmful interactions with students of color, that often result in exclusion, when the teacher moves away from the humiliation model of "classroom management."

Arguably, even reprimanding a student with an even-toned or friendly voice, from an authoritative position, at the front of the room while students are in a seated position, is still a form of public humiliation. We know that teens have a deep-rooted need to feel accepted by their peers. The use of humiliation is an abuse of teen dignity as it capitalizes, directly, on the most vulnerable aspect of this developmental period; humiliating a student publically, even with a simple remark, attacks their developmental need for acceptance rather than supporting them by bringing them back into the group.

And let's remember how the dynamics of race and gender identity play in. Harmful cultural expectations for African American and Latino boys dictate that they could be viewed as a punk or sell-out if they display obedience to the control of authority; rather, they may gain cultural currency for displays of (perceived) bravery and disobedience to authority. The answer, then, is not to shout louder, humiliate, or find better ways to manage one's tone of voice to frighten or control. Continued conflicts over small acts of disobedience, nationally, lead to the outrageous statistics above—students are finally ejected from class so that some imagined network of control inside the school environment can teach the students a lesson. After this doesn't work, the child is once again turned over to a higher source of authority—often the U.S. prison system.

We Resolve to Make It Better

Here are resolutions that we, as educators, can take to end the cycle of racist humiliation from inside our classrooms. It all starts with a few promises and new skills:

1. I will no longer use my school's disciplinary referral system, unless a student actually wields a knife or gun, or is publicly ingesting drugs or alcohol right in front of me. I believe in my ability to do this.
2. I will examine my practice daily to review the places where I used humiliation and control to manage my environment.
3. I will discard my hoped-for facade of control and perfection. I will be willing to apologize for my actions and show myself as a human being who makes mistakes.
4. I am willing to use a new skill set to work with students, which may require me to feel discomfort as I shed the tools of humiliation that were also used to control me.
5. I will work toward handing more power over to my students while artfully working to provide them with opportunities to gain skills needed for higher education.
6. I will provide more visual reminders of anti-racist philosophy, while also working inside myself to eradicate my own need for total control, especially over Black and Brown children. I will acknowledge and work through my fear of losing control.
7. I will fight against archaic discipline policies that I am expected to follow because of poor leadership. I will reject punitive systems that promote institutionalized racism and speak out to request new

systems. *Bonus—students will notice that you are
doing this and appreciate you for it!*

8. I will place my desire for each child's trust above
   my desire for control.
9. I will look for and assume the presence of a
   unique brilliance in each young person, including
   Special Education students.
10. I will accept that many students of color have
    experienced trauma throughout their education
    before coming to my class. I will build my class-
    room to be a place of healing and possibility.

To genuinely adopt and enact the above promises, educators and administrators can post them and review them
each day. Parents and community members can share them
with leadership teams at their neighborhood schools. I use
them as tools of self-examination to improve my practice
and continuously try to eradicate elements of control from
my teaching. The results, for me, have been transformative.
I regularly develop and maintain wonderful relationships
with students that continue long beyond the time that I
have them in class; I do not write disciplinary referrals;
students see my classroom as a refuge from the dynamics
of institutionalized racism and power and control—and
they respect the classroom environment even more for that.

But the work goes beyond adopting a list of ten agree-
ments. One must also develop a set of tools and skills that
create instruction based on tenets other than control and
humiliation. What, then, is this new pedagogical philosophy
based on? It is based on *surrender, relinquishing power and
control, valuing the individual, creating space* for students
to speak, listen, and learn safely, and creating *intriguing
curriculum,* that beckons their curiosity, that they desire

and value the opportunity to learn what you have to offer.

Only you can remember that unique reason why you fell in love with physics, or why protecting the natural environment led you to become an AP Environmental Science teacher, or why poetry kept you alive, or how the art room was the sacred space that saved your life. To be an outstanding educator, your passion for your subject area has to come out of you every single day. Every single period, sparks must fly to light up the young minds that have come into your presence hungry to learn (don't let apathetic faces or focus on cell phones fool you; they honestly wish to be challenged and turned on to new ideas and skills). What an enormous job you have chosen. If you have the love for your subject area—you have the most meaningful ingredient.

To best share your passion and your dedication to equity with all students without humiliation, you incorporate the *surrender, relinquishing power and control,* valuing the individual, *creating space* for students to speak, listen, and learn safely that I mentioned above. It's probably not as hard as you might think.

How to Build a Culture of Respect without Humiliation

Before trying to employ these techniques, we all must take the time to ask what kind of energy and attitudes we are bringing into the classroom. The work required for legitimately understanding energy is a lifelong process—one that I am still engaged in on a daily basis. Adopting an undeniably positive attitude toward being an educator and toward young people only requires an intellectual understanding and a willingness to embrace a new perspective. Most of us already come with a very noble and altruistic desire—the desire to serve. The problem, for many white educators, occurs when that desire faces off with years of institutionalized racism that operates inside the system, causing distrust in our students. Additionally, few teacher education programs offer classes about eradicating institutionalized racism from schools. Classroom management classes continue to provide solutions based on subtle humiliation. Teachers enter with the right desire, but with inadequate skills to support that noble desire.

The technique and attitude that I propose emerge from experience, and from my work as a yoga teacher. I engaged in an intense (five nights per week minimum) period of devotion to yoga during my initial years as a teacher. Every problem that I faced in the classroom, I brought to the mat. I experienced being inadequately equipped to deal with the diversity, the anger, the indignation, and the desire to rebel that I saw in my students. The problem, for me, was that I was extremely rebellious when I was in high school too. I intimately understood the students that now saw me as an authority figure to disobey. I felt the daily loss of my best intentions.

But I continued to bow down on my mat, pray, and meditate, listening for an answer. Around that time I made the decision and commitment to see what would happen if I dedicated all of my life's energy to teaching. Back in the classroom, I started to see that the answer was about being aware of my body language and my words. I noticed that students always reacted with disdain if I called them out for something in front of the whole group; I committed to never admonish a student in front of the entire class. I used the act of surrender, bowing down, that is so crucial in yoga; I applied it to my relationships with my students.

I began to view myself, during class time, as a being who was, indeed, there to serve them. Viewing myself this way meant (literally) on a regular basis, going down to my knees to speak with students at their desks. Some students, especially those who had been scathed by humiliating tactics in the past, needed to see me take this friendly, service-oriented approach over and over again. Some students even tested me to see if they could get me to admonish them in front of the whole class. Sometimes I wasn't perfect, but they could see me trying to do things differently, and they loved it. Also, I wasn't just treating the Black and Brown students this way; this was the way I was treating every student in the environment.

Then, I considered the methods of the most influential teachers. I asked, in meditation, what it earnestly meant to be a skillful teacher. I realized that if, when I went to a student's desk to kneel down and speak with them about getting on track with the work, I addressed them individually with a compelling question, I could thoughtfully honor the legacy of the most influential teachers. To do this, I had to intently think about the reading assignments so that I always had a set of challenging questions to bring to any student who was off track. The environment is controlled by intellectual stimulation, challenging questions, personalized instruction, and surrender of control.

In conjunction with this approach, I give instructions to the whole group at the start of class with a powerful, direct, confident voice. I provide extremely comprehensive directions that are written on the wall, written on a small assignment sheet at their desks, and I offer them verbally as well. Then, after I have given them, I automatically go to each table group to check for understanding.

The surrender technique comes in when a few students are slightly off track. The individual challenge questions or additional help with understanding the original question, asked from a position lower than eye level where I am, physically show my willingness to surrender power to keep students focused.

How to Start

Start through self-observation. Take the time to observe yourself for a day. Carry a clipboard and monitor the number of times that you overtly admonish or verbally redirect your students in front of the whole group. How many times did you do it? How did you feel about yourself as an authority figure when you repeatedly admonished young people? Do you want to repeat these feelings for thirty years? What if you never, or rarely, had to do this? Do a bit of writing about what you found.

Now pick one class, maybe one of your less demanding to start, and set a boundary for yourself. *I will not admonish any single student in front of the whole group during this class period.* Carrying your clipboard will be crucial during this time. Make notes about any students that you see off track. Make sure you are moving around the classroom. Feel free to walk near these students, and make a note on your clipboard; doing this alone may make a difference. If you feel ready, kneel or crouch down to redirect through a question in a low voice. It will be easiest if you begin using this technique at the start of the year. If you are transforming your practice, remember that students will continue to test you to see if they can get you to go back to the old way. The technique will also be ineffective if your curriculum is not challenging and intriguing enough, or if your original directions were not extremely clear.

Some teachers may not feel comfortable kneeling or crouching down to place the student's eye level above their own. Obviously, there is another way to make this happen. You can ask the students to stand up and have a talk with you, looking at them at eye level (or slightly below). Helping students to feel comfortable in the room means that they may stand up when they need to. Also, if they have a question, they are not stuck at their desk, they are empowered to go to you to seek the answer to that question. Does this mean that students can be mulling around the room all of the time? If the learning activity allows space for movement, then yes. If the learning activity requires seated work, then students should still feel comfortable getting up to move their body at any time.

When you get those elements in tune, you will see that you can produce an environment where students enjoy learning. You can create trust with your students. In a situation where a student is absolutely off track, you can still use the technique to speak calmly with them by calling the student over to talk to you at your desk about what is going on that day. Ask them to sit in a chair next to you at your desk so that you can speak with them away from the group, eye to eye in a seated position. Doing this will reduce the anger that comes from being taken out into the hall; talking in a seated position, either next to one another or eye to eye, promotes a feeling that you care about what is going on. First, listen. The five minutes that you take away from the whole group will pay off when you win the trust of this student. If your table groups are well-balanced and your assignment was clear enough, you should be able to have these types of conversations during class anytime you wish without fearing the loss of control.

Now you have two techniques to use that will help you to avoid getting into a scenario where you use humiliation and end up sending students out of class because they cannot jive with your ineffective systems of control. If you never admonish students in front of the whole group, students will feel very comfortable in your room. If you change your body language and tone of voice, quietly questioning students about their understanding of the subject matter when they are off track, and genuinely asking them if they need any more help to solve the problem, you will see your students getting on track. If you commit to repeat, repeat, repeat these techniques, the students will begin to trust that they can ask you questions about your subject matter and learn from you.

If you carve out a place in your room for seated-not-heated semi-private conversations, you will have a custom system for dealing with the underlying issues that can sometimes cause problems. You will find out that your students are hungry, facing trauma at times in their homes, exhausted from too many activities, struggling with self-confidence, and a million other personal dilemmas. When you listen, when you redirect, asking students if they can return to their work just for today after you have listened to them (and possibly provided them with a granola bar), you will find courage in the place of that rebellious anger and stress that they directed towards you, as the authority figure.

Administrators can help to eradicate the culture of humiliation by giving teachers the space and time needed to realize that this culture exists. Making time for teachers to read this chapter during professional development is a good start. Administrators may help educators become conscious of the power and control dynamics by setting up role plays during staff development with a team of willing teachers. During the role plays teachers will demonstrate how humiliation can take place in the classroom environment, and then provide a healthy example of how to relate to students without humiliation. Administrators can also record the voices of students who have experienced exclusion and humiliation so that teachers can hear, first-hand, how the students are impacted.

The work of helping teachers to understand, however, is only a small part of the battle. Teachers who have operated their classrooms through the use of humiliation will often be resistant to change. Administrators must be willing enough to require that this shift takes place. Likewise, unions must fully support administrators who are actively working to eradicate racism from the classroom environment. With or without union support, administrators can choose only to hire educators who understand the concept of removing humiliation and exclusion from their classrooms or show a distinct desire to learn. Veteran teachers who refuse to investigate how power and control operate in their classroom environments must not be called "proficient" or even "developing" during their annual review. Administrators must be unwavering enough to call out deficiencies while offering sincere support. In some cases, teachers who refuse to alter their practices to eradicate racism must be removed from the classroom and encouraged toward an alternative profession. Administrators can empower themselves and gain a stronger base of support in the following ways:

1. Reach out to union leadership and request the opportunity to have coffee during the summer or at the start of the year. Engage in an ongoing

discussion about racism and exclusion that occurs at the classroom level. Bring a supportive parent or two to this meeting to clarify your position and ensure that you have a witness.

2. Build a strong base of support in your school community through offering support to excellent educators who engage in non-racist practice. Show support through the power of positive reflections, notes, as well as opportunities to lead. Bring great teachers together to set a standard of excellence in your school community.

3. Bring parents of color in through monthly dinners where you offer real opportunities for parents to express their activism. Encourage letter-writing or in-person dialogue with educators. Let parents know that you will be meeting with the union representatives to discuss racism and exclusion in the school environment. Invite them to come along.

How Can Parents and Community Members Help to Dismantle the Culture of Humiliation and Racism:

1. Parents and community members can make a powerful impact by requesting the opportunity to meet with administrative staff to find out who, if anyone, in their school environment is engaged in equity work. Parents can request information on how they can help to push this work forward. This is not the work of parents of color only; it is the work of all parents and community members who wish to end racism in schools. In fact, parents of color have complained about the racist treatment of their children for decades. It is high time for white parents to make this a top priority!

2. Administrators are often burdened with so much work that they must respond to the fire that needs to be put out on any given day. Parents can make racial equity a priority by, essentially, forcing the issue. Working together in teams, parents can call or email to find out what exact measures are being taken to reduce inequity in the school environment. They can apply pressure so that the issue of basic human rights is the first priority in the school environment.

3. Parents and community members can request the opportunity to meet with union leadership. While parents are often directed to make complaints to the school board, they rarely deal directly with union leadership. The union leadership must be amenable to the request for these types of meetings, as they must uphold the image that the students and families are their top priority. In meetings with union leadership, parents and community members can demand that administrators be allowed to do the work of holding teachers accountable for exclusion that takes place inside the classroom. Doing so is not an attack on educators; voicing concerns about teachers who refuse to change their practices must be viewed as an act in favor of human rights.

A well-run classroom can be a refuge. It is a refuge for broken hearts. It is the place where students come when other teachers or administrators humiliate them. It is a place where they come when they don't have class—just to put their head down on the desk for a moment to catch their breath. It is a place they wish to use for their club meetings, to eat lunch, to do a bit of homework from another class, to imagine a different world.

4

Teaching Transformed

PARENTS AND COMMUNITY MEMBERS:

To better understand the origin of institutionalized racism at the classroom level, it is critical to recognize the effect that corporate control of educational standards has on curriculum design. We must see how the needs of students of color often go unseen in the curriculum, instruction, and assessment, and how the reality of an 82% white teaching force translates to discriminatory curriculum design.

How Corporate Control of the Testing Structure Upholds Racism in Curriculum Design

Standardization. The word alone implies the exact erasure of individual identity that it sadly causes in real life. To create tests that school districts can sell nationwide, companies like Pearson, Harcourt Educational Measurement, Riverside Publishing (a Houghton-Mifflin Company), and CTB McGraw-Hill must develop tests that assume a knowledge-base that is full of implicit bias that benefits white Americans. In other words, to sell the test, these companies must create questions that will be as useful in a conservative state like Arizona as they are in a liberal state like Vermont. The common denominator in the construction of these tests is Euro-Americentric content that is easily transferable from Florida to New York, and from California to South Carolina—the common denominator being *clarity to white children*. Implicit bias doesn't just slip in; implicit bias is the very fabric of these tests. The assumption that one test could measure students with such diverse language backgrounds, knowledge bases and learning styles is ludicrous. These tests further embed implicit bias into the curriculum of overwhelmed educators trying to prepare their students for the test.

The homogenization of curriculum design that happens due to the domination of standardized testing giants leads to teachers sacrificing their creative freedom; and to the lack of inclusion of the histories, pedagogical needs, and experiences of children of color. Even when efforts are made to include one or two passages on a Language Arts or Social Studies examination by an author of color, token passages do not and cannot reflect the diversity of the nation's classrooms. Furthermore, this sense of tokenism does not encourage teachers to consider substantial shifts in curriculum design or pedagogy. If they are required to prepare students for the test, if they have accepted the position of teacher in a state that operates, like most states, in the mill of required-state-testing-to-qualify-for-state-and-federal-funding, they have no reason to diverge much from the status quo—Euro-Americentric curriculum that promotes a white supremacist version of history as innocuously as an airborne illness.

Our schools have been handed over to the testing system. Test-makers make enormous sums when they contract with states to provide assessments and assessment data, and students of color and students living in poverty are grist for the mill. The rhetoric of "closing the achievement gap" might as well be promotional material for the aforementioned assessment firms. The gap is sold as the chasm of knowledge between white students and students of color. The measurement of this gap is now part of the corporate rhetoric of the big data machine. I am not suggesting that we, as educators and community members, wouldn't want to know about the "achievement gap," but as it stands, the testing corporations are paid millions upon millions, while little funding is channeled towards direct services for students of color and students living in poverty to rectify systemic inequities. For example, while millions are spent annually on testing

Portland Public Schools, there are no programs available to provide additional preparation in science and mathematics during the summer to students of color, who often fall behind in these areas by seventh grade, making it thereby impossible to reach the highest levels of AP/IB mathematics or science by the time they reach high school. Per middle school, summer Bridge programs could be offered at the rate of $10,000 per school—a total of less than $200,000 annually for an entire district to help rectify inequities and make it possible for students of color to enter high school on a more level playing field in terms of knowledge and skills in these important STEM areas.

The role of parents and community members is absolutely crucial to solving these problems. Parents can help by acting as watchdogs for the district, as well as voicing their opinions on how funding should be spent. One main reason testing corporations have such tremendous power and influence is because they were able to sink their teeth into state boards of education, which have little public oversight. Parents must band together to request public documents, examine spending, and call out the names of those who make behind-the-scenes deals with big data at the expense of genuine education. Technology can be a great tool in states where these decisions are made at the state capitol—parents can readily discover who to email regarding budget and assessment questions. Similarly, parents and community members can have a louder voice in local spending on education by attending school board meetings and finding ways to develop political action committees where they share information, act as a unified force, and target a number of strategic issues—placing eradicating racism from the public system at the top of the list. By acting as watchdogs against inequity, by banding together to make it a priority, the voices of groups that are currently isolated from one another can be instead strengthened by each other's presence. Black, Latino, and Native American parents groups must band together; and white parents too must place equity as a top priority—as the only alternative is to continue to promote a system of inequity that, one hundred years from now, will be remembered like South Africa's Apartheid. This is no exaggeration. Readers must notice the decrepit conditions in Detroit Public Schools, while schools not too far away in Grand Rapids have excellent ratings. Whether due to discrimination based on neighborhood, discrimination that occurs through tracking students of color into lower-level courses, or discrimination that happens inside the classroom, students of color are consistently pushed into substandard educational conditions and their white peers are not. This consistent separation into a lower tier life, based on race and class, is precisely what I refer to when I say Apartheid. The reality that many people feign ignorance when the discussion about racism in education occurs is belied by the protests some community members participate in when a suggestion is made to blend more students of color into a high performing, traditionally white school, or to remove barriers from an AP program. Skeptics, consider speaking out against racism in a public forum or attending a school board meeting to request support for students of color rather than testing. You will feel the resistance that arises from standing for children of color. Skeptics may begin to understand the reality that these children themselves walk through every day as they navigate extremely racist environments.

Diverse groups of parents that include parents of color and white parents can be most effective in demanding change from school districts and state boards of education. Parents must work together first to identify the nature of racist inequity that occurs in their district, collaborate to decide how to approach the problem in a systematic manner, and develop strategies for persistently and even aggressively naming leaders who promote inequity through buying into big data testing. All parents must act as watchdogs, ensuring that state and district funds are directly going to services for students, and services that provide oversight to guarantee serious efforts are being made to offer additional opportunities for students of color to gain the skills and mentoring they need to be successful.

Curricular Revolution

At the start of my career, I yelled a lot. I am a small white woman with a thin frame. This is not an excuse, just a description. I didn't have many of the skills I have now with regard to curricular organization, "classroom management," etc. I was young. At the time, the thought of trying to control my students, especially larger males of color, seemed daunting. I was just learning to use stories to engage young people. I was already developing some meaningful relationships but did not completely understand how to surrender. So when things felt out of control, I would raise my voice to its highest pitch. It was such a shocking shift from my usual smiling face that it stopped my students dead in their tracks. I must have seemed unhinged.

But my students loved me through it. One day, after a wild yelling session, one of my students, a strong, sweet boy from a Pacific Islander background, came up to me while the students were leaving class. I'm sure my face was still red from fury.

He said, "Open your hand."

I opened my hand. He placed a long string of shells in my hand.

"Ms. Bartley," he said softly, "Don't yell. It's bad for you in here."

He pointed to his heart, smiled sweetly, and left.

I never yelled again. For the rest of my career, I surrendered that. Something about the way he told me that, the shells, the idea that this peaceful soul was watching me—it irrevocably changed me in that moment.

Of course, I had to do the work of figuring out what to do instead of yelling. I chose to do that work. This is what I mean by surrendering and letting the students guide you. It was contextually inappropriate to yell at my students; eroded any chances of establishing a stable level of trust. Yelling was how I was taught to control people. But, my student's kindness encouraged me to stop yelling, and I am so grateful that he did. This moment sparked an internal discussion and process of self-reflection regarding my entire modus operandi. I took the time to consider the ways that my curriculum itself reflected control. I accepted that my routines, modes of control, and anything I do in the classroom, is part of my curriculum. Students are continually receiving messages from me about what it means to be educated, how they deserve to be treated, and what it means to be an authority figure. The moment my student gave me those seashells helped me to take more responsibility for my curriculum, and to accept a much broader definition of curriculum—a definition that combines my *methods* for transferring information to students and *how* I am sharing that.

As we open this discussion on letting go of behaviors that are rooted in white supremacy and/or inappropriate for one's context, we must know and respect that educators of color can uniquely connect to non-white students. Though educators of color still have to work hard to understand the populations they serve, they relate with non-white students (even if students are from different cultural communities) in one fundamental way: they share the experience of living in a society that privileges white people. They share the experience of operating inside the school environment built on institutional racism. Stereotypes and racial bias show up differently for different cultural groups, but educators of color have a common experience with students of color in that they, most likely, have experienced racism in an educational setting and society at large sometime in their life, or perhaps their day.

I share this nuance to show that we *all* have work to do to serve our students. White people are not *doing extra work* by studying student populations. Educators, who wish to excel, must study student populations throughout the entirety of their careers (because populations are steadily shifting). All non-white teachers must do this too. And people of color have to do the extra work, throughout their lives and inside the school environment, of dealing with institutional racism. Sometimes (too often), educators of color are burdened with the additional responsibility of educating white peers about their culture for no extra pay. In my personal experience, white teachers will be appreciated much more by their fellow educators of color if they do not make them responsible for their cultural or racial education.

Many educators of color will appreciate the chance to talk openly about the racism they see. They will appreciate you even more if, over a period of years, you show yourself to be a genuine accomplice who is willing to stand up against racism in the school environment. In many school environments, educators of color may not feel safe in being the first to speak against the racism they see and experience. White teachers can use their white privilege to voice concerns; in my experience, educators of color who may not wish to be the first to speak will be the first to back you up if what you say is authentic and sincere. It may take months or years of repeated anti-racist work to gain trust, but over time, I hope you see and feel the same collegial trust. These relationships are what move the work of far-reaching equality forward.

In addition to helping me to stop yelling, my student taught me an invaluable lesson about operating a culturally appropriate classroom. While I grew up with a certain amount of yelling, it was inappropriate and strange for a good number of the students that I served. My student, Chris, challenged me to ask myself this question: *If I am not going to raise my voice in a desperate plea for dominance and control, how am I going to redesign my curriculum and teaching methodologies to operate in a manner that creates a more harmonious and culturally appropriate environment?* Engaging this question was by no means easy, but humbling myself in pursuit of the answer was the best choice. Not just because I am still in touch with Chris, but because it prompted me to open the door to a world of learning about the meaning of a peaceful and productive environment in a variety of cultures. After learning about the creation/maintenance of peaceful and productive spaces in several cultures, I dared to ask questions about the meaning of excellence and success in a variety of cultures. From here, an array of individual conversations enlightened me to how poverty, race, gender, and sexuality intersect to create barriers for students. A beautiful aspect of doing this work is in finding out how a student's individual culture can become a source of strength to challenge the system's obstacles. In spite of the beauty and witnessing students challenging obstacles, this work still does not eradicate racism. We must use activist education too, removing the obstacles that exist in schools while helping students to contextualize the barriers they face in society. If we stand in solidarity as teachers, administrators, and community members, we can create a new system that, instead of setting up hurdles for students to jump over, launches students into the world well-prepared.

A revolutionized approach to education that is devoid of racism will require us to reconceive of the very meaning of curriculum design. If we are honest, we must admit that we know many teachers who continue to recycle curriculum each year. Some, due to total exhaustion at the end of each day, never look back to reconsider what worked and what didn't. A colossal impediment to racism-free schools is the notion that the authority, grading system, and curriculum design of the teacher should not be questioned. There are many teachers who regularly reassess their work, reconsider their strategies, and work toward full inclusion of the cultural community that they teach. However, I am aware of another demographic of teachers who operate from an antiquated respectability politics standpoint—that the teacher is to be respected, and furthermore, questions about his or her curriculum design or methods are an attack to the teacher's professionalism. This idea, operant inside the 82% white teaching force, breeds another form of institutionalized racism—authoritarian power tripping. The system operates on a construct of the teacher as *master* of knowledge, methodology, and assessment. The notion of teacher as master connotes that the other people in the room, the students, are of lesser value. Arguably, the term "master" evokes the collective memory of enslavement or at least colonial oppression. The notion of the teacher, alone, holding the reins of power and control is coupled with oppressive curriculum and discipline strategies, further exacerbating authoritarian educational dynamics. The system and its constructs are bound to fail when we reconsider that 82% of U.S. teachers are white, and students of color constitute more than 50% of our school population, nationally. In this light, the concept of teacher as the master is inconceivably racist. There is a movement, however, away from this ideology.

To excel in curriculum design within the context of a public school, teachers, community members, and administrators must arm ourselves with an understanding of how privilege plays into the way that teachers design curriculum, and how the concept of teaching and learning works in the homes of the students we teach.

If you haven't already, read everything written by education advocate, Pedro Noguera. Noguera is the foremost living scholar and researcher on issues facing students of color, particularly African American and Latino youth. There is no way to reduce his work to one quote. His transformative ideas, if embraced, can help to inform and educate the 82% so that we are adequately equipped with the skills and knowledge to serve our students. Of course, Noguera is a proponent of ensuring that there are role models of color available for young people of color. If there is one lesson that I have taken away from Noguera, it is that we must continually re-examine both the macro and micro aspects of our system, uprooting institutionalized racism at both the federal and classroom level if we wish to, honestly, be a nation with democratic ideals. Here is a link to Noguera's blog: http://www.pedronoguera.com/blog/

Likewise, authors who are interested in alternative views on curriculum design should subscribe to the Rethinking Schools Magazine, which will help to connect you with excellent alternative ideas about curriculum design. The Zinn Education Project (www.zinnedproject.org) is another reliable, well-organized resource to find teaching materials that support social and racial justice in schools.

A positive ideology to replace the teacher as a master

paradigm is, the teacher as an activist concept. Adopting this self-concept requires that educators submit to the constant reassessment of the power and privilege dynamics in one's classroom and school environment. By any means necessary, educators must be willing to play an active role in ending racism, holding an openness to learn more— both from students themselves and from other activists. Understanding one's school population is a pre-requisite to becoming an activist educator. The work of understanding a school's ethnic and racial demographics is crucial to complete before working to transform curriculum—as we must know who we are serving to offer excellent lessons and build a deliberate connection to our students. This work is not limited to teachers—it is pertinent work for administrators and parents as well. The following passage offers some questions for self-reflection, as well as questions to understand your school population.

Understand Your School's Demographic

Before curriculum planning, investigate your school's population and gain a keen understanding of the backgrounds of the individual students you are teaching. Make sure that you hold a vision of *who your students* are up with what you plan to teach.

I realize that it sounds tough to tailor a curriculum that serves both your Pacific Islander population and your African American population, but this is what we need to do. We must know our population to serve them adequately. Some educational consultants that I have come across through professional development experiences inaccurately portray meeting the needs of diverse populations as learning to serve Black and Latino students, only. My suggestion is to study the exact ethnic demographics that you serve and learn as much specific information as you can about the various populations in your school environment.

Knowing general information about "Mexican American" culture is not specific enough. Mexico is an incredibly diverse country with multiple language and cultural groups. China too contains hundreds of religious and geographic nuances. Students who are classified as "African" have national and cultural identities that are not visible on the computer screen that tells you about their ethnic background. The systemic denial of these nuances in our method of recording and communicating information is, in fact, an example of whitewashing, or promoting a disrespectful and racist blindness.

In my experience thus far, students have been thrilled to share about their specific cultural practices; all have appreciated my desire to see them for who they are, and not for how they are labeled. But it is also unfair to make the student responsible for your cultural education. You can also learn about the cultures represented in your school community by seeking that information on your own. You can do this through reading, visiting cultural centers and restaurants in your school community, and if invited to a cultural event in a student's home or at a community center—go! You will have far more success if you do your research and try each day to gain more knowledge about the communities that you are serving.

Questions for Reflection:

Some central questions to begin to better understand your school population are:

1. What is the ethnic breakdown of my school?

2. What is the socio-economic breakdown of my school?
3. What neighborhood do most students in my school live in? Do I live near my students? If not, can I take a long walk there?
4. What are the major cultural institutions in the neighborhood(s) where my students live?
5. Who are the community leaders among my students?
6. What are the best cheap restaurants in the neighborhood where my students live?
7. What kind of work do the parents of my students do?
8. What kind of crime is operant in the neighborhoods where my students live?
9. How does the underground economy work in the community that I serve?
10. What kind of music do the students I serve listen to? Do I know about popular musicians for each group I serve?
11. What are the expectations around gender in the communities that I serve?
12. How do families operate among the communities that I serve?

As demographics change throughout the United States, the answers to these questions can change from year to year. One is never "done" with the process of learning about the myriad of cultures in their community. For all educators, I think there is one more critical aspect to accept—teachers of color also have to do the work of learning about their student population. Being a teacher of color of Latin American heritage, for example, does not give one any specific knowledge of the experiences inside the home or cultural community of Vietnamese students. We all must engage in the work of knowing one another.

Visiting cultural centers, taking classes in cultural studies, developing a passion for learning about the cuisine in your students' homes are all fun and exciting ways to start learning about your student population. However, learning about different cultures does not mean we won't come out valuing our home culture more. That is the problem with the concept of multi-culturalism. In some ways, it provides a way for whites to show that they were non-racist by appreciating, visiting, and mimicking other people's cultures. But these actions are not exclusively non-racist because they don't actively challenge racism.

The question to grapple with is—*how do I go beyond multi-cultural appreciation to a place where I change my attitude so that I, indisputably, believe that my values, views, perceptions of reality are not superior to others?* A process of self-reflection is required here. Here are several questions that educators in the 82% can benefit from, but that non-white educators who serve populations different than their home culture may also find useful:

1. What kinds of art, music, and literature was I taught to value in my home environment? Am I tacitly promoting the culture of my home culture? Does the literature in my classroom reflect the students that I serve? What kinds of art, music, and literature do my students experience and celebrate in their home culture? Have I taken the time to find out?

2. What political values was I taught to value in my home? Do I assume that I should omit politics

from the classroom, but, in practice, tacitly promote my values by pretending to be devoid of political perspective? Am I aware of the political perspectives and experiences of my students? How could I learn about that?

3. Where did my attitude about school discipline come from? Was exclusion used against me as a punishment in my home? Was humiliation used? Do I believe that others should suffer the way that I suffered? Do I believe that my tactics are less harsh than the tactics I experienced in school or at home? Thus, they are more just? What are my discipline tactics? What would be my ideal discipline system, if I could design a just system? What do my students feel a just discipline system would look like? How could I find out?

4. What are my spiritual beliefs? As a public school educator, I am aware that it is not appropriate for me to bring these out into the classroom forum. Still, my religious beliefs may impact my values. What are my deepest beliefs? Am I aware of the religious backgrounds and spiritual views of my students? How could I learn about these? How might my classroom practices and discussions invite in conversations related to faith and spirituality without breaking the law?

These questions could also be fodder for a start-of-the-year survey through which you find out crucial information about your students. It is always okay to allow students to omit an answer on this kind of survey if they feel the questions are too personal. And it is vital to get beyond the need to survey by having real conversations with students.

The crucial takeaway is that we, as educators (especially if we are members of the 82% who do not have the experience of living as a non-white person in the United States (your mission trip to Mexico doesn't count as a time when you were a minority)). We must be willing to look at the places where we are clinging to the values that promote white supremacy. We need to let them go. In my experience, it is not difficult to see where these places in ourselves are; for they are places where we become enraged with classic white rage (or maybe little twinges of fear and anger) when they are challenged. This rage is what causes the thousands of disciplinary referrals for "minor disruptions" or "insubordination". Instead of turning that rage into punishment, what if we saw ourselves in our fear of losing our sense of authority and surrendered to a new way of teaching—letting the students guide us is a place to start. Taking the time to do the above exploration exercise can help with the complex process of analyzing which of our curricular elements or classroom practices may have unconsciously supported our own values, rather than welcoming the perspectives and values of the populations we serve into the process and the product.

The knowledge that you gain through becoming a student of the cultural communities that you serve can greatly impact the way that you design your curriculum. There are so many levels to the ways in which your curriculum design will shift as you better understand your population, including:

1. You will understand the meaning of school for each cultural community, *which will inform the way you communicate with families and design your pedagogical framework.*

2. You will understand the way stories, images, and ideas are communicated in the cultures you serve, *which will enhance the way you communicate your lessons in your classroom.*

3. You will understand the academic vocabulary that you may need to pre-teach in order to best serve your population, *which will allow you to create greater equality by including all learners.*

4. You will understand how homework may or may not fit into the lifestyle of your students, *which will impact the amount of homework you assign, and/or the way in which you communicate your expectations to families.*

5. You will understand how to compliment a student in a way that will be most beneficial and culturally appropriate, *which will help you to establish stronger relationships with your students.*

6. You will understand how feedback is given in the different cultural communities you serve, *which will help you to understand when to use a more direct approach and when a more indirect approach will be preferable.*

7. You will understand the tools your population may have access to, and which you may need to provide, *which will help you to pre-plan so that your students have access to the resources they need to be successful.*

8. You will understand the skills and knowledge your students may be equipped with, and which you will need to pre-teach, *which will inform the way in which you design your lessons.*

9. You will become aware of and include a variety of new texts, videos, guest speakers, etc., that you can involve in your curriculum, *which will make*

your curriculum far more dynamic, intriguing, and effective.

10. You will understand a variety of new modes of expression that can be used as assessment options to show understanding of learning goals, *which will make your students more likely to be engaged.*

The suggestions that I make here require critical thinking, emotional and ideological adjustment, and change. This work is essential to the process of renovating curriculum design. Administrators can support teachers in this work in the following ways:

1. Create information sheets on the school's community for teachers to review at the start of each year.
2. Provide access to afterschool language and culture courses for teachers. Or, utilize part of the professional development time to provide language and cultural courses.
3. Provide time for teachers to work on curriculum redesign with the goal of more equitable and inclusive curriculum. Teachers spend a great deal of time, by administrative request, on preparing the curriculum to meet the state testing standards. Shift the focus toward equity and inclusion. Allow teachers who excel to present their work.
4. Allow students, parents, and community members to take part in leading professional development. Parents can be boundless resources to help teachers and administrators learn about cultural expectations, needs, definitions of school, and expectations for success. Students themselves, since they are of a different generation of their parents, must be granted the opportunity to define the meaning

of success for themselves. Self-definition is essential to ensuring barriers that are related to gender and sexuality are navigable.

5. Students live in a different world than their parents, yet they must understand both the expectations of their cultural community, their parents, and their teachers. Ensure that students have the space to explore the varying sets of expectations that they experience. Give students the space to share their inner conflicts, as well as their hopes and dreams, with teachers.

As we move forward as educators and community members, curriculum design can no longer occur in a vacuum that is separate from the multiple worlds that students are living in. Tangible knowledge of our students must be part of curriculum design. In fact, students' knowledge of one another can and must be part of the actual curriculum to traverse the boundaries of race, class, gender, and economics that are part of the landscape of public schools. In every discipline, we must allow students to be people before they are pupils. Making space in the school year for getting to know one another (beyond the surface level) not just on the first day of school, but throughout the progression of one's education, is essential for the acquisition of deep knowledge and personal empowerment.

Parents and Community Members:

Aforementioned in Chapter 1, to transform our system, the inclusion of adults of color is crucial. Parent-teacher associations (PTA) are dominated by, upper-middle-class, often white female parents, who, by virtue of their power and privilege, have the free time to commit themselves to serving in their school community. The overwhelming presence of white parents becomes problematic in a public setting because the needs and demands of these parents take priority over the needs of children whose parents do not have the privilege of being involved in school decisions. Some PTA groups attempt to remedy this by working to include parents of color in the group. This is a start, but it will not be effective if token parents of color are still out-voiced by dominant white parents.

At one school, for example, I noticed that many years and hundreds of thousands of dollars were spent by the school community to prepare for the senior all-night party, an event designed to keep students safe from drunk driving after graduation. The planning committee, each year, met many times to carefully execute this expensive event, which still cost about $50 per student. Meanwhile, many other pressing needs, like the exclusion of students of color and hyper-policing of students of color, were never addressed. Furthermore, students living in poverty could not even attend the event, which visibly catered to the needs of the children of upper-middle-class parents. I do not write this to shame these parents, but to ask readers to analyze how power and privilege play out in your community's PTA. Parents can support the revolution for anti-racist public education by ensuring that schools hire teachers and staff members of color. Often, parents have the opportunity to take part in the hiring process, both for principals and teachers. A second tactic is for parents to request information on how these teachers will be supported by the administration.

White parents operating in exclusion cannot make a positive contribution to ending Apartheid in public education. Many wish to support schools, even by donating money that they would otherwise send to a private institution; at the same time, they feel entitled to have a say in how the school spends these funds. This sense of entitlement is rooted in white supremacist ideology. Parents should not be expected to donate to public education; nor should they be allowed to gain power based on donations, *money they chose to give*. Following this logic, parents can also help by lobbying for more federal support of public education, working to surrender their voices to promote the voices of parents of color, and never expecting that their financial donations come with strings attached that improve the quality of education for their own children.

I wish to encourage parents of color to operate with the same sense of entitlement as many white parents; however, I regularly observe how the public school apparatus rejects or ignores parents of color who express themselves, at the same time embracing and praising white parents who express their power through donations and posterity. This is not to say that all parents of color are impoverished or do not make donations—many do; however, I continue to see white parents who make donations at the helm of influence and privilege in public education, from Portland to Westchester. The remedy? White parents who are willing to recognize the operation of white supremacy in schools must, in fact, refuse to make further donations and band together behind parents of color and parents living in poverty until schools address the latent issues impacting families of color. There is no single answer to the long-term dilemma of white supremacy in schools, but dismantling its economic backdrop and shifting power toward voices of parents and community members of color could produce a needed wake-up call. The alternative is knowingly accepting that white parents participate in Apartheid. Everyone has choices. What choice will you make?

Clarity as a Tool for Equity

Along with understanding who your students are, clarity is
another essential tool for successfully teaching in diverse
environments. Institutional racism thrives on the absence
of clarity regarding which rules apply to whom and what
those rules are.

Institutional racism thrives because schools are places
that have been established to foster and protect white Anglo
values and modes of existence. Nationally, exclusionary
discipline happens at significantly higher rates to children of color (starting in kindergarten), in part, because,
in addition to the Puritanical values of white supremacy
being rigidly upheld, largely by white educators, there is
also a complete lack of clarity regarding many aspects of
classroom communication.

This part of the text is about how clarity can lead to
stronger relationships and more equitable environments.
Students who are non-native English speakers and students
from traditionally marginalized backgrounds need to know
exactly what they are expected to do. They also need to
know exactly how to ask for clarity, *and they need to be
made to feel comfortable asking for clarity without feeling
as though they are insulting the teacher for not being clear.*

For every assignment, especially when you are teaching
a new skill, continue to ask yourself if you have made the
assignment clear to all students through auditory and visual
communication. As soon as they are in their work groups
or working individually on the assignment that you have
made clear, *wander around the room and check with every
single student* at their desk or table group to make sure they
understand—and do it without making them feel stupid.

How do you check in with every student without making them feel that you are patronizing them? Before you move around the room and ask them to get started working, you simply announce that you will be coming around to check that they understand the assignment. Take notes. If a student asks you a question always say, "*Great question!*" Make it a little bit audible in the room so that students know you are happiest when you are being asked questions, even if they are simple questions that help them to comprehend the assignment.

Asking questions is a huge sign of trust, especially for students from marginalized backgrounds. If you are asked a question by a student, especially about clarity, allow yourself to feel a twinge of joy—for you are building the essential trust that students need to build useful skills for life. You are building academic confidence, a pivotal life skill that will help them through college and beyond. You are a precious asset in their lives if you can do this. Let them know how honored you are to be asked.

Always be available to make the assignments and expectations clear. All year. Every assignment. Same technique. They will love to see you move around and treat everyone with matching levels of respect. Questions will bloom like flowers. A classroom where students feel comfortable and safe to ask questions is a successful classroom.

This technique also has, within it, a strategy that can help to prevent exclusionary discipline. Since students know you will be moving around the classroom to check for understanding, and that you are a teacher who communicates with every student every day, you can use an "understanding check" as a behavior assessment tool for a student who appears to be acting out.

For example, maybe you think you see a student peeking at another student's paper, or you see one student speaking to another student during a moment where they are supposed to be working. Instead of going straight to punishment mode, go straight to understanding check mode. Don't do it in a mean way. Don't fear your student. Go over and gently ask if they understand the assignment. Or, if you already know they understand the assignment, ask what problem they are on. Take that attitude of wanting to work through the problem or sentence or equation with the student for a few minutes. Direct their attention away from the power struggle and right back to their work. Challenge them mentally to see if they can apply their mind to the work and get props from you for solving the problem. They will respect you a little more after that because you showed the ability to keep your cool and keep focused on the work. *They will also be less likely to act out, as they know you are coming over—not to punish them but to give them an intellectual challenge.*

Don't ever use the understanding check technique to humiliate the student in front of the group. Do this quietly just with the student to help them find their inner logical problem solver. This makes learning fun for both of you… but you do have to be on top of your curricular game to do this successfully.

Let Every Child Know that You See Them

Make eye to eye contact and have a conversation, albeit brief, with every student every day. Some of the best teachers I know check in with every single kid each day at the start of class. Each student has to give a one-word answer or an adjective to describe their weekend or their previous

ortland. He excelled, graduated, and went
y intact.

ere is that it is imperative for educators to be
t damaging, and to educate ourselves about
that exist to attract first-generation college
students of color. It is never okay to project
vard a student based on assumptions or old
Many colleges now pride themselves on pro-
holistic admissions processes. If you are not
practice is to help the student to contact the
e of admissions to ask about opportunities for
on students and students of color. I sometimes
t call for them, to model how to proceed. Then,
m to make the other calls.

get an answer, I've been known to get parent
nd take the student to the campus to meet with
officers in person. In fact, I can't think of a year
ive years when I have not done this. It is a real-
hetimes the parents of first-generation college
l not feel comfortable going to a college campus
y not be able to take the time away from work).
dents who are brilliant and homeless, or brilliant
political refugees who worked day and night.
ping to take them to the college campus? Nobody,
is is not a white savior story. It's a statement to
cate that sometimes *we* (a collective "we" that
ducators of all races) do have to go the extra mile,
dred miles, to rectify racial and socio-economic
when we see it setting up roadblocks in students'
e I ever driven a first-generation student (with
rmission) to meet with an admissions officer?
times than I can count. Have I ever driven an

evening. I prefer having a brief conversation with students while I am walking from desk to desk to check their work.

In addition to speaking with them at their desks, I call students over for three-minute private meetings at my desk. The purpose of my meetings is often to go over one of their goals (while also checking in about skills), either for my class or their year as a whole; I use this time to check in about classwork and focus juniors and seniors on their academic goals and the college application process.

Yes, we would hope that high school counselors were able to do this kind of goal setting with students. The reality, as many of you already know, is that many counselors are inundated with either scheduling or helping students through arduous personal issues. These two aspects of their work often take up 95% of their time, not allowing them to have reliable relationships with all of the students on their caseload. To support counselors' work, I often use goal cards. I have an index card for each student that I keep in a box. After one-on-one meetings, I take notes on students' cards about their goals, and I set a half an hour meeting with each counselor where we can go over 50 to 90 student goal cards. At this point, there is no risk of too many teachers using this strategy (as I have never met another who does). However, if it becomes a national trend (which I hope it will), departments will need to decide which teacher will be working with which students in support of the counselors. We are not at that point yet, so I highly recommend trying out this strategy in your classroom to give students additional mentorship that they genuinely need. I try to have these meetings with counselors at least once per week, but this is not always possible. When they are possible, these meetings allow for excellent communication and great collaboration regarding student goals and needs.

Starting the goal card technique is simple. At the start of the year, I pass out the cards and ask students to write their name and personal cell phone number on their card. I tell the students the exact parameters under which I would use that number. I would only ever text or call them for two reasons: 1) I need to try to communicate with them about an issue or problem, and I am willing to work it out with them before going to their parent. 2) I need to contact them about a scholarship or internship opportunity. I always call from the school phone, not my personal cell phone so that they do not have my number. I always directly tell the students that I will never call for creepy reasons like hanging out or going out for coffee. Students laugh at this, but I know they appreciate it and trust me more, as there are some creepy people out there who harbor ill intentions towards young people.

I also ask them to include information about their future plans and collegiate goals. I ask them to write the colleges or community colleges that they are considering on the card. Since many of my students will be first-generation college students, I invite them to write me a note if they have no idea which colleges to consider and need help. In my experience, students are very grateful for the chance to reveal this privately; they are equally grateful to know what options exist for them.

Remember, this is all about building rapport with students to teach them and empower them. Clarity and encouragement are important here, especially with students of color who are underrepresented in college student bodies and who may not have other people to guide them through the college admissions process. Students need to understand that their

GPA and test score
are clear with ther
students will be m
admissions proces
their story or situati
applicants as well as
cation essays. And it
aid opportunities tha

Sadly, I have see
crushed the dreams
telling them that their
a gentleman claiming
to our school to volun
Latino students, Aleja
legiate goals. The volu
test scores and told him
goal for him. My stud
ing that many private c
holistically (many are w
examinations in lieu of
all but kicked this guy's

My student applied t
sity of Portland to study
to both. Of course, Alex'
he apply to five or more
dream of attending colleg
asked him to give up that
to Reed College. Even if he
been better for him to go th
failing. Supporting student
ing them off before they try
work. Due to a superior sch

University of
with his dignit
My point h
supportive, n
opportunities
students and
negativity to
information.
viding more
sure, the bes
college's offic
first-generati
make the firs
I sit with the
If I don't
permission
admissions
in the past
ity that son
students wi
(or they m
I've had stu
children o
Who was g
but me. Th
communi
includes e
or one hur
injustice
lives. Ha
parent pe
Yes. Mor

evening. I prefer having a brief conversation with students while I am walking from desk to desk to check their work.

In addition to speaking with them at their desks, I call students over for three-minute private meetings at my desk. The purpose of my meetings is often to go over one of their goals (while also checking in about skills), either for my class or their year as a whole; I use this time to check in about classwork and focus juniors and seniors on their academic goals and the college application process.

Yes, we would hope that high school counselors were able to do this kind of goal setting with students. The reality, as many of you already know, is that many counselors are inundated with either scheduling or helping students through arduous personal issues. These two aspects of their work often take up 95% of their time, not allowing them to have reliable relationships with all of the students on their caseload. To support counselors' work, I often use goal cards. I have an index card for each student that I keep in a box. After one-on-one meetings, I take notes on students' cards about their goals, and I set a half an hour meeting with each counselor where we can go over 50 to 90 student goal cards. At this point, there is no risk of too many teachers using this strategy (as I have never met another who does). However, if it becomes a national trend (which I hope it will), departments will need to decide which teacher will be working with which students in support of the counselors. We are not at that point yet, so I highly recommend trying out this strategy in your classroom to give students additional mentorship that they genuinely need. I try to have these meetings with counselors at least once per week, but this is not always possible. When they are possible, these meetings allow for excellent communication and great collaboration regarding student goals and needs.

Starting the goal card technique is simple. At the start of the year, I pass out the cards and ask students to write their name and personal cell phone number on their card. I tell the students the exact parameters under which I would use that number. I would only ever text or call them for two reasons: 1) I need to try to communicate with them about an issue or problem, and I am willing to work it out with them before going to their parent. 2) I need to contact them about a scholarship or internship opportunity. I always call from the school phone, not my personal cell phone so that they do not have my number. I always directly tell the students that I will never call for creepy reasons like hanging out or going out for coffee. Students laugh at this, but I know they appreciate it and trust me more, as there are some creepy people out there who harbor ill intentions towards young people.

I also ask them to include information about their future plans and collegiate goals. I ask them to write the colleges or community colleges that they are considering on the card. Since many of my students will be first-generation college students, I invite them to write me a note if they have no idea which colleges to consider and need help. In my experience, students are very grateful for the chance to reveal this privately; they are equally grateful to know what options exist for them.

Remember, this is all about building rapport with students to teach them and empower them. Clarity and encouragement are important here, especially with students of color who are underrepresented in college student bodies and who may not have other people to guide them through the college admissions process. Students need to understand that their

GPA and test scores are elements of college admissions. If we are clear with them about this, starting in 7th or 8th grade, students will be more likely to be prepared for the rigorous admissions process. They also need to know what about their story or situation will help them stand out among other applicants as well as how to write about them in their application essays. And it's crucial that they learn about financial aid opportunities that they may qualify for.

Sadly, I have seen cases where fellow educators nearly crushed the dreams of first-generation college students by telling them that their dream was not possible. Not long ago, a gentleman claiming to be a retired college counselor came to our school to volunteer his services. One of my brilliant Latino students, Alejandro, met with him to discuss his collegiate goals. The volunteer college counselor looked at his test scores and told him that Reed College was an unrealistic goal for him. My student came to me, distraught. Knowing that many private colleges look at young people more holistically (many are willing to consider excellence on AP examinations in lieu of high SAT scores), I was furious. I all but kicked this guy's ass. And he was incorrect.

My student applied to Reed College and to the University of Portland to study pre-medicine. He was accepted to both. Of course, Alex's counselor and I suggested that he apply to five or more colleges, ensuring 100% that his dream of attending college would happen—but we never asked him to give up that bigger dream of being accepted to Reed College. Even if he had not gotten in, it would have been better for him to go through the process of trying and failing. Supporting students on that mountain, not knocking them off before they try is the theory at the heart of this work. Due to a superior scholarship, he chose to attend the

University of Portland. He excelled, graduated, and went with his dignity intact.

My point here is that it is imperative for educators to be supportive, not damaging, and to educate ourselves about opportunities that exist to attract first-generation college students and students of color. It is never okay to project negativity toward a student based on assumptions or old information. Many colleges now pride themselves on providing more holistic admissions processes. If you are not sure, the best practice is to help the student to contact the college's office of admissions to ask about opportunities for first-generation students and students of color. I sometimes make the first call for them, to model how to proceed. Then, I sit with them to make the other calls.

If I don't get an answer, I've been known to get parent permission and take the student to the campus to meet with admissions officers in person. In fact, I can't think of a year in the past five years when I have not done this. It is a reality that sometimes the parents of first-generation college students will not feel comfortable going to a college campus (or they may not be able to take the time away from work). I've had students who are brilliant and homeless, or brilliant children of political refugees who worked day and night. Who was going to take them to the college campus? Nobody, but me. This is not a white savior story. It's a statement to communicate that sometimes *we* (a collective "we" that includes educators of all races) do have to go the extra mile, or one hundred miles, to rectify racial and socio-economic injustice when we see it setting up roadblocks in students' lives. Have I ever driven a first-generation student (with parent permission) to meet with an admissions officer? Yes. More times than I can count. Have I ever driven an

18-year-old-student who had no legal guardian, in my car, to a college campus? Yes, friends. On every single occasion, it has been the right thing to do.

Always be clear with words and boundaries, both with students and their parents. On parent night, make sure to clearly explain the reasons why you would contact their child so that parents are aware of the reason for your communication and your professional boundaries. I would want this for my child, *but what are your unique expectations and needs*? In my experience, parents and students alike appreciate clear communication, both in terms of daily classroom directions and long-term goals.

If we are to transform schools to become places where students from non-white backgrounds can thrive, we must be willing to surrender our desire for power and control in the classroom. Be very clear about our goals and expectations, and provide *faithful encouragement* that lights the path to realities that may have been impossible for the previous generation. This usually requires conversations with each child (and their family if possible) regarding what they expect for themselves. When students set expectations and goals for themselves, and when we honestly believe (no matter what obstacles may make a dream seem impossible) in a student's dream, that vision becomes the best rationale for them to put in the work daily.

Questions for Reflection:

The *faithful encouragement* that shows students multiple pathways to their goal, whatever that goal is, is a crucial key to developing excellent rapport. *What would it be like to, in addition to being a source of knowledge and instruction, to be a source of encouragement and faith?* Take some time to write about that. In what ways are you already providing faithful encouragement? In what ways do you believe that sharing your toughness and sarcasm with students will best prepare them for life's hard, cold, realities? Our most riveting stories—the stories about places where we failed and got back up—are far more persuasive to young ears than sarcasm and toughness. Blending your sincere wisdom, with clear goal-setting, and a "you can" attitude is like a cure for classroom apathy, disenchantment, and marginalization. How could you increase your encouragement for every child this school year? Adding faithful encouragement into your daily practice towards your students will bolster your relationships with your students.

Note to Administrators and Policymakers:

The suggestions for teachers included in this chapter are of little consequence without the support of administrative and district leadership teams who are ready and willing to find ways to allow time for the essential work of transforming teaching methods. Supportive administrators and district leaders could re-engage teachers who possess an antiquated pattern of curriculum recycling and power-tripping if these teachers were required to and provided time to, restructure their teaching. Teachers are facing increased workloads, as well as increased testing and paperwork expectations—none of which help us to address the racism in our system. We need district leaders who are willing to dedicate substantial professional development time to teachers. With this support, the teachers can begin the process of self-reflection needed to understand their own supremacy, explore the populations they serve, and revamp curriculum to guarantee that they are updating their methods to ensure clarity and recognition of each child's presence in the room.

Teachers need to be accountable for doing the work. One way to assist teachers in moving forward would be to require teachers to individually answer the questions provided in this book during professional development and hand in their answers. Reviewing their answers may seem impossible given the flurry of activity at the start of the year, but this practice will help those tasked with educational *management* to empathize with the absurd schedules that many teaching staff face, while also trying to keep up with assignments.

Note to Administrators and Policymakers:

Administrators, please take the time to answer these questions yourself. Field trips into the community with your entire staff, processing demographic research with your staff, and showing your willingness to share your answers, will help you to shine as a transformational leader who is willing to dig in and participate in the revolution for greater equity. In the next section of Part II, you will see an argument against hierarchical structures in classrooms. Please read this section, as it is part and parcel to a larger conversation about the failure of hierarchical models for district leadership that is continued in Part III of this book. In short, if we want teachers to engage with students on the premise that all human beings are of equal value, how can we reconsider the ways that the structures of schools themselves (with administrators at the helm and teachers beneath) reproduce ideologies of supremacy?

Radical Change Requires Everyone

The work of restructuring public education is not the sole responsibility of teachers, parents, community members, or administrators. All must engage in the process. All members of the society must collectively become conscious of the mass oppression that is taking place. All must accept the choice to redesign the system; no one, even those who send their children to private school, can dispossess themselves from the responsibility of ending Apartheid. We must attempt to examine this historical moment with the eyes of the historians of the future. They will look back and see the reality of mass incarceration of people of color; in fact, the school-to-prison pipeline is already well-documented by historians and sociologists who work for our federal government. History requires us to make a choice to stand against Apartheid or own the responsibility for a crime against humanity. Moving against Apartheid must shift the dynamics in every PTA meeting. It must alter the rhetoric of every policymaker. It must shake the walls of every school board meeting. It must be the sole priority of every policy maker and administrator. It must take place in every classroom—and it must be the conversation in every staff room. The energy required to eradicate racism must be stronger than the greed of for-profit prisons; it must be more powerful than the ubiquitous denial of white privilege; it must be more forceful than white rage; it must be more demanding than the priorities of wealthy white parents. *What it cannot be anymore is patient.* The truly patient, by nature, will wait forever. White power, by nature, will never surrender. The time is now, to decide that patience can no longer supersede justice. We must act in solidarity on behalf of justice to manifest a different vision of education.

5

Building Peer Relationships for Equity

While the previous chapters focused on techniques for building equity in your classroom, those of us dedicated to eradicating institutional racism must, of course, take the revolution beyond the classroom. We must unite with our fellow teachers, counselors, support staff, and administrators who are also working to promote equity so we can, one day, change the whole system. The ways we find allies in the mission to transform our schools for equity and racial justice will vary depending on geography, teaching culture, school climate, institutional memory, and other elements of organizational psychology that impact how we operate as communities of educators. The first step, as is almost always the case, is to observe.

Over many years of observation, I found that in most high schools throughout the United States, there is one distinct group of teachers that has a lunch clutch in the staff room every day at. They have been having lunch together so long that they each have their armchair or spot on the couch where they normally sit. This is not an indictment of this group of educators. I have often gone in to these spaces to observe what goes on.

On the surface, they are the nicest group of educators you could ever meet. In one school that I observed, each holds (or has held) an additional responsibility at the school, making contributions to athletics, arts, etc. When they get together, they take a few moments to talk about elements of white American popular culture like movies, television, or news. The problem is, the main group is all white; and, up to this point, there has been no other meeting space for teachers who do not wish to commune to talk about these exact topics. The group will be kind to anyone who enters; that is not the problem. The problem is that the one community center for educators in the school building is monopolized by a single group of veteran educators who have established a pattern of discussion during the one moment in the day when teachers and staff members could be coming together to address problems of institutional racism and inequity that are taking place in our school environment. Educators who are not white or who are white activist educators who wish to transform the system, and do not wish to discuss issues related to popular television shows or films aimed at white audiences, would have to surrender aspects of their selves in order to join in. This climate would require educators of color to assimilate with the white group in order to eat lunch in the staff room. This dynamic promotes the dominant culture while silencing the movement for radical transformation. The subtle and seemingly innocuous conversations about the popular culture of the hegemony help to maintain white supremacy and its associated culture of blindness to injustice.

Questions for Reflection:

1. Where do teachers convene in my school? Does one group of white educators convene to socialize,

excluding (unintentionally) teachers of color or teachers who do not fit the mold? Take a moment to describe the organization of teacher cliques in your school.

2. What do teachers tend to talk about when they convene inside the school building?

3. To what extent are teachers conscious of the inequity in my school environment?

4. To what extent do teachers in my school play an active role in demanding system transformation toward racial equality?

5. To what extent do teachers spend time complaining about students or their families?

6. To what extent do teachers include or exclude teachers of color?

7. Who are the teachers or staff members in my school environment who are excluded or isolated from cliques of teachers who band together?

Facilitate Change

I am certain that what I am describing does not take place in every school across the United States, but I am willing to bet that a similar dynamic pervades most U.S. school staff rooms. The fact that our teaching force is 82% white impacts the school environment for students, as we've seen, but it also creates an environment of white supremacy that affects fellow teachers. But it doesn't have to be that way. There are steps you can take to help facilitate a shift toward equity in your school's culture beyond your classroom.

Research Racism

In an effort to share perspectives that are not commonly heard in the staff room, or in other areas of the school that are white dominated (which is pretty much every area of the average U.S. high school), here are a series of questions for administrators to privately ask educators of color, so that administrations can better understand the work environment and remedy inequity felt by staff. Teachers and community members must also be concerned with the answers to these questions and can encourage the administration to address them, but it is important to ensure that staff of color are not pressured to publically address them without additional pay for their time. The system must pay staff of color for additional time they spend researching, explaining, or clarifying the nature of inequitable conditions. Otherwise, they are once again being asked to complete additional work while also experiencing racism in the workplace. Here are potential questions that could be helpful to inquire about, perhaps through a survey, on paid time for the staff of color:

1. Have you ever felt that you were expected to assimilate to aspects of white culture in the school environment where you work? If so, where do you feel this the most? Can you please share about how this feels for you?

2. Where and with whom do you eat lunch? Do you avoid the staff room at your school during lunch? Why? What features could make that environment more comfortable for you?

3. Have you had experiences with racist staff members, ranging from micro-aggressions to overt racism, in your experience as an educator? Please describe those experiences.

4. How do you identify your allies, both as an employee and as an agent of change in the movement for equity in public education?

5. What advice would you share with an incoming staff member of color about surviving and thriving as a public school employee?
6. Noting that the U.S. teaching force is 82% white, what would you like white educators to be aware of and/or change to create a more comfortable working environment?

You cannot just ask these questions in a survey or casual conversation. Most staff members of color are going to need to have a certain level of trust in you before they discuss how they are marginalized at work. Some may need to see some action or non-racist work on your part before they are willing to have this kind of conversation with you. When you show up for the Black Student Union meeting (or host it in your room), participate in Latino club, etc. you take steps toward having trusting relationships with staff members of color. After you establish that trust, you, in a private location, can ask about their experience. Finally, you can begin the work of forming a long-term relationship by offering and providing authentic support when they experience that marginalization. They may or may not call on you, but will most likely appreciate having an ally, even to vent to. Whatever you do, don't put anyone on blast, meaning—do not take an issue that was discussed with you privately and make it your crusade without the permission of the person who suffered. Rather, maintain that relationship over time and ask them how you can be a support. When called on, do what they ask you to. This humble approach will make for more powerful change and better long-term relationships with staff members of color.

My own experience of finding allies and accomplices, as an outspoken, white activist educator who entered teaching with the primary goal of continuing the battle for racial justice in public education, could be useful. Though I have an apparent layer of power and privilege that commands a greater ease, in finding allies and establishing relationships. With this note on privilege, I'll share a few techniques that I have used to identify allies.

Use White Privilege to Spy

I learned one of my most important lessons about building relationships and finding accomplices through my former mentor Dr. Charles Hopson. When I had overheard a racist comment by a fellow white staff member and came to him to share about it, Dr. Hopson encouraged me not to disassociate with this individual.

"What you just had, Susie," he said, "was a privileged conversation. You don't want to get rid of those relationships; you need to keep them."

It took me years to stop getting furious at white racism and listen to the advice of my mentor. Now I get it. Being white allows me an exclusive window into the world of overt white racism that people of color may not be directly exposed to, though they will feel the results of racist attitudes most acutely. Whites who are openly racist in front of other whites will often pretend to be kind, genuine, and non-racist toward people of color in public. Dr. Hopson encouraged me to use my whiteness to be a spy, but to keep my heart and my feet firmly rooted in the revolution. I am still amazed by his calculated, methodical view of people and relationships; I also see that only by virtue of my whiteness could I walk through professional life *without* such a calculated view.

What do you do with the information you have gleaned from spying? You take a look at your staff list and carefully make notes on the attitudes towards race that you experience around you. By making notes on people who have shown racist attitudes over time, you can more clearly see *who is not your ally.* You'll also notice which of your colleagues respond to racist comments with non-condoning silence or outright dissension. These people very well could be your greatest accomplices. You are building, foremost, an informed team of movers and shakers who want to alter the environment.

Identify the Flock

For any institution to function, there have to be those individuals who simply follow along with the status quo. As we now know, the status quo of discipline and pedagogy in the United States does promote racism. But I am talking about a core group of people at your school, some of whom may not intend to uphold racism—some of whom may even be people of color (though this is less likely in my experience). People who tend to follow directions and rarely, if ever, shake the boat or question the flow of the institution can become crucial advocates for change if *you and a group of committed educators and administrators are able to change the status quo.*

If the dominant culture of a school becomes focused on anti-racist work, then that same flock who followed the expectations set by school leaders will become advocates for anti-racist work. Many may have wished for solutions but did not have the courage or wherewithal to rebel on their own. Do not write anyone off quickly. You may see changes in people if you are willing to put forth the courage and get with some badass changemakers.

Find Your Heart Team

Finding genuine accomplices is about more than just political agreement. For me, true accomplices in this work are people that I prize above my best friends in life—they are more than friends; they are people who are willing to take risks and fight for students with me. Genuine allies are people ready to make sacrifices for the common goal of fighting racism and other forms of social inequity that impact students. When I started my career, I was looking for people who were willing to work with me on a revolutionary approach; my expectations were close to gangster—I was looking for loyalty, sacrifice, willingness to change the system by any means necessary.

I found out that everyone is not Malcolm X and neither was I. It hurt when a person who was an acomplice on one issue was nowhere to be found on another. As I matured, I realized that being an ally requires mutual understanding about the lengths that the other person is willing to go, what issues are most important to each, and what needs for confidentiality or recognition each party has. Having unrealistic expectations that accomplices will speak out publically against the district or administration will leave you friendless, but realizing that each person can contribute in their unique way and pace will make you an effective leader. Great alignment also requires a willingness to support other people's causes and interests. Though few people are interested in relationships of intimate loyalty to social revolution with their work colleagues, most do appreciate the opportunity to contribute to the betterment of society; most also value relationships based on reciprocity. Genuine accomplices, the kind who are willing to make distinct sacrifices toward the greater goal, are few and far between. How do you find these solid comrades who understand the urgent need for change?

Sometimes, you find your heart team when you are crying in the bathroom after a student is sent to jail. Sometimes, you catch another teacher in your arms after they have tried everything and lost a student to the streets or suicide. Sometimes, the weight of district mandates bearing down on all of you will create a unique solidarity; and in that, you'll hear a courageous voice emerge in a staff meeting. Often, the students themselves will help you to see who your accomplices are. They will show you where they feel comfortable, who they respect.

As a sports team has players in different positions, your heart team will have various players as well. They'll range from teachers to administrators to parents to the students themselves.

Teachers as Activists

Consider this: most teachers, if they make it past their first four years, tend to stay between twenty and thirty years; whereas the average principal or vice principal leaves after three or four years. Teachers have a long-term stake in schools; we are there to execute a vision that we who stay continue to construct together. The members of your heart team will appear in various manifestations; take the time to embrace them, listen to them, and collaborate. These crucial relationships between teachers are our greatest hope for major institutional transformation.

So take the time to converse with your fellow teachers. Take a chance—bring up the inequity you see in your school's AP Program or discipline policy. Listen to what they say. Is your fellow teacher open to the idea that all students, if properly challenged and supported, can achieve at a college level? When you bring up this idea, do they support it, or do they come up with a litany of excuses as to why college is not for everyone? Do they have a gatekeeper mentality or an equity-focused outlook? If they have an equity-focused outlook, they may be as hungry as you are for the chance to collaborate and work to take a wrecking ball to the gates, within your school culture, which are preventing all students from reaching their highest potential. Perhaps you will decide that your common issue is the removal of school police from the main hallway of the school during lunch. As a leader, it could be a good idea to select three issues related to eradicating racism that you would like to organize around, and then try to get a sense of which you can gain the most support behind. Even better, consider which issues impact the students of color most. You can create a survey for students and parents of color. You do not need permission from your administration to ask questions to your students or your parents; nor can you be punished for it. Sharing the results of this inquiry with other teachers can be a great way to gain momentum as well, as many teachers do care sincerely about the students and may feel it most effective for students to bring the issue to the forefront.

After taking a few months to get to know your fellow teachers, make a list of those who you feel may be prepared to collaborate as racial justice collaborators. Number the list from 1-20, least to strongest accomplice. Foster your relationships by sharing articles, eating lunch together, proposing texts to read over the summer, and taking advantage of opportunities to attend alternative professional development opportunities that support the work you wish to do.

Conference for Radical Educators and Community Members:

The Teaching for Social Justice North West Conference happens in Seattle or Portland each October. Teachers and community members are welcome to come and learn from activist educators on a variety of fascinating topics. Attending will put you in touch with a remarkable community of activists who wish to transform the system.

Activist Administrators?

While the term *activist administrator* seems like an oxymoron, and they are, admittedly, scarce, I am fortunate to know a few. Finding your equity-focused administrators is imperative. While activist administrators are busy, they are never too busy to speak with teachers who have ideas about how to improve the quality of education for all students at their school. As you did with your fellow teachers, you must find out which of your administrators are equity-focused.

Observe how administrators deal with discipline. Do they look the other way when inordinate numbers of Black and Latino students are brought to the principal's office, or do they come up with alternative strategies to solve discipline problems that may also originate from a school or teaching culture that feels like a hostile environment for students of those cultures?

Observe how they run professional development and weekly meetings. Is equity a priority they speak up about and focus on? If the meeting is about equity, is there one particular administrator or principal who seems to take the lead on those occasions? Forge a relationship with this administrator.

Request a fifteen-minute meeting with this administrator to share your vision and ask how you may be of service to his or her equity goals. Explain ways you feel the teaching culture can be changed; share how the administration can be of support to you in shifting the culture. Also, ask for a list of teachers or school staff who they would suggest you speak with about your equity goals. You are not doing this to kiss ass or to gain power in the school environment. Be about service.

After you have forged relationships with a few other activist teachers who are practicing differentiation and scaffolding for diverse groups of students, teaching academic vocabulary to support college-level work, and using other strategies designed to empower all students, ask your administrator to allow your group to share these innovative strategies at a staff meeting as part of your professional development plan. This group of teachers can role-model new "norms" for the rest of the group; thereby acting as catalysts in the process of shifting the school culture. If there are naysayers among the teachers in the audience, prepare ahead of time with your network of equity-focused teachers so that you have a strategic plan (and evidence) to support the strategies that you suggest.

Students

Another crucial element in the process of cultural transformation involves fostering the voices of your student role-models. Attend your Black Student Union, Latino Student Union, Asian and Pacific Islander Student Union meetings, and any other student groups that represent the needs of marginalized groups in your school (though they may even be groups that represent a large population of students who

128   A DIFFERENT VISION

are still marginalized by institutional racism in the school culture). Meet the presidents and vice presidents of each organization. Allow one of these groups to meet in your room each week. Donate to each.

If you have made a connection, consider asking the students to help with a few survey questions about the experience they have as a student of color at the school. Specifically, ask them if they feel that they are expected to take the most challenging courses available at the school and if they feel that they are expected to attend college.

Also, ask them if there are a few teachers or counselors or any other school staff members who have encouraged them. Allow them to use names for this part. These individuals are allies to build networks with.

Parents

Finding your parent allies in the PTSA is essential for a complete cultural transformation. Attend the PTSA meetings, or at least attend one or two. The parents will be thrilled to see you showing up to support their important work. Take a look around. Which communities of color are represented in your PTSA? Listen and learn. Is equity an issue that your PTSA is interested in addressing? Are there allies that you can make in this group?

Your PTSA community is the place where you will find parents who are true believers in public education; however, as previously discussed, you may also find that those who hold multiple privileges comprise the large percentage of the group. Among the PTSA parents are also people who are willing to spend the evening at school, even though they may have worked all day themselves. They are people who are gathered together for the sole purpose of improving the school. You may find your most reliable allies in this group, especially if you can listen for voices that express concern regarding inequity—and those who keep the focus on transforming the system for increased racial justice.

Reach out to your parent communities of color. If your parents of color are not in the PTSA, then where are they? At some schools, the PTSA will contain parents of all ethnic backgrounds; however, many studies have questioned the ways that PTSAs can be gatekeepers for equity by unintentionally (or intentionally) marginalizing parents of color. If the PTSA at your school is predominantly white parents, ask if there are any culturally specific parent organizations, like a Latino parent group. If specific parent groups exist, like a Latino parent group, it is necessary to inquire about their purpose and efficacy. Do they have the same political capital as the PTSA? Efforts to blend them into the PTSA may weaken their power to make an impact in their desired manner while causing discomfort. How can their intention be preserved and their group empowered? If they wish to, can they meet on their own and still have a vote on issues that impact the school PTSA? Is there any reason why they should have to change their meeting time and methods just to blend in with the traditionally whiter group? How can you as a teacher help to empower them?

If no such groups exist, ask the PTSA if they would be willing to do some outreach to invite more parents of color into the PTSA. Teachers can be extremely helpful in spreading the word by making copies of invites, using district translation services to get documents translated, and ensuring that parents of color get the news about meeting dates. Otherwise, PTSA groups often rely on email lists that come from meetings that were traditionally populated by white parents and the exclusion continues. Helping to disseminate information is a simple, but a crucial form of advocacy.

Activist Administrators Build Bridges

Administrators can take a decisive role in supporting the development of more equitable parent and teacher relationships. One of the best strategies that I have seen for building community when two great administrators of color, Shay James and Ivonne Dibblee. The two transformed the old, dreary "back-to-school night" into a community bar-b-cue where the teachers were tasked with meeting and greeting parents while everyone enjoyed food and beverages in a relaxed, outdoor setting. Coming from work, parents could relax and get to know the teaching staff. Translators waited at the entrance to ensure that families had the help that they needed. Instead of sitting in a forced, formal meeting in each teacher's classroom, parents could wander the halls to look around, conversing with teachers more naturally while kids played in a bounce house. Parents and staff applauded the administrators who revised parent night. Teachers found time to convene with one another, and even to converse with administrators and other school staff members in a setting that promoted feelings of equality and positivity. Changing long-term practices and traditions requires courage and collaboration, but can yield excellent results.

The key ideological shift that I hope this chapter will produce is that ending teacher isolation is an essential step in the process of creating more equitable schools. We must find ways to reach out beyond our classrooms, work with fellow teachers, administrators, and educational partners in our schools to build a movement that will transform schools through the synergistic collaboration of diverse professionals who are skilled in different ways. I learned this the hard way—by coming in like a lone soldier and trying to break it down all by myself. We cannot shift the whole landscape unless we have a team that works together.

This perspective requires administrators to place their role as public servants above the role of leader, and for teachers to accept administrators as fellow public servants who have a different role. This is easier said than done, as administrators are often placed in the position of oppressor when state and federal budget limitations continue to cut into the heart of the work. Unions must continue to lobby for more funding for education, to reduce class sizes and teaching loads, and to demand opportunities for authentic professional development and teacher mentoring programs that allow us to move forward as a solid team. Administrators must be willing to step away from antiquated practices that promote and maintain white supremacy if they wish to earn the honor of being known as an *activist administrator*. They must sometimes sacrifice the illusion of power to empower their teacher and parent communities. They must also have the courage to represent the community that they serve, even when their plans do not match with an off-target district, state, or federal vision. This vision of synergy between parents and school staff and the intention to increase the leadership and teaching positions of staff of color will help us to transform public schools, finally moving toward system transformation.

6

Facing Fatigue: How to Stay Sane While at War

There have been a few moments in my teaching career that were so hard that thinking of them brings a tear to my eye. I remember the day my student Fernando Chavez, a bright Mexican American young man, surviving despite incredibly difficult familial challenges, was shot and killed by an intruder to the home that he was staying in as a guest. Fernando had stepped out to protect the home and was shot and killed by the intruder almost immediately. The investigation revealed that his murderer was a metham-phetamine-addled burglar looking for a fix. Fernando was brilliant. Fernando was putting every effort toward scaling the numerous obstacles stacked before him. Fernando was one of the funniest young people I've ever met. Fernando is gone forever.

There have also been many successes. I remember the countless hours of work that went into mentoring and sup-porting my former student, Mike Mengistu in his college application process. Mike's family had emigrated from Ethi-opia; though his father was well-educated there, the family was not familiar with the nuts and bolts of the application process in the United States. Mike believed he could get into MIT. He started preparing for this dream by engaging in internships and additional learning experiences during his sophomore year of high school. During the end of his junior year and throughout the start of his senior year of high school, Mike came to see me for more than twenty-five private meetings to fine edit his applications. He applied early and was told that his application was deferred and would be considered in the regular admission process. We went back to the drawing board, figured out what additional materials he could send and waited. When Mike was officially accepted to MIT with a major scholarship, his mother came to my house with a parade of incredible Ethiopian delicacies. I had the honor of experiencing the beauty of Portland's Ethiopian community as they came together at the Mengistu household to celebrate Mike's achievement, and later his sister Amen's acceptance to the University of Portland with a Black United Fund scholarship. The joy that I experienced with this family, and many others with similar stories, is a priceless gift that I cherish.

Sometimes there are smaller gifts for me to cherish. I had a student this year who struggled with organization. Kim Z. was incredibly creative, and a phenomenal abstract thinker, but the level of abstraction that was comfortable for her made it very hard for her to write an essay in a linear way. I sat down with Kim and her mother to discuss strategies. I told her that I was going to write a general outline in the margins of her papers for a few weeks, and then ask her to fill in paragraphs based on my notes. Soon, she was using this technique to organize herself. By the end of the year, she passed the AP exam with a 4, an excellent score; furthermore, I know that she will go to college with the skills she needs to organize her essays. I have the privilege of helping young people gain life-changing skills, and for that I am grateful.

For the most part, my relationships with students do not cause me great fatigue—usually, they are a source of hope, faith, and inspiration. I do feel fatigued, at times, when dealing with the racism and *racists* in the system. Yes, I said it. Eduardo Bonilla-Silva, in his book *Racism without Racists: Color-Blind Racism and the Persistence of Racial Inequality in the United States* questions the routine I see daily in schools—teachers and administrators realize that inequality exists inside the school and system, but most are dumbfounded at the idea that they may be perpetuating the racism. Eradicating racism in one's self is a lifetime pursuit; the battle to eradicate it from the system as a whole will extend beyond my lifetime. Still, it can be lonely, frustrating, and difficult to experience hatred from those who are too scared to face it at all. Resistance is expected. Many people, teachers included, are blind to the omnipresence of racism and do not have any desire to change the system. Tools of self-care must be employed to continue to press forward in the battle for social justice, especially if you are in a population of educators who are still unable to see themselves as vectors of racism or even see the racism operating all around them.

Investing Yourself

Exemplary teaching requires a level of commitment, to each child, which necessitates that we shapeshift between the apex and zenith of our emotional capacity, on a daily a basis. I am not talking about playing the role of social worker for each student. However, meritorious teachers become *invested* in the students' progress in class. This investment in each student's knowledge and academic development is fundamental to the shift that needs to take place in public education; likewise, the investment in the battle against systemic racism is crucial to the transformation toward equality in public education. Teachers who are engaged in passionately working toward social justice while concurrently giving themselves unconditionally to 180 students can easily head toward a total breakdown.

Many teachers with great potential, often those who are willing to invest into the work emotionally, are the first to depart from the profession. The truth is—you can spend all of your emotional, creative, and spiritual energy in service of your astounding students and toward greater equality in your school environment, but (other than your compensation package) nobody is going to take care of you when you shatter. Other teachers are trying to stay afloat. Our friends in other professions may try to understand (but in the back of their minds wonder why we are complaining when we have the summer off). Administrators are focusing on student-centered issues, parent and community relationships, funding, and systematic concerns. The only person who can take care of you is the woman or man in the mirror.

In addition to the dramatic and emotionally wrought experiences brought to us by our relationships with hundreds of students, teachers are also on the front line of the battle for funding in public education. Every two to three years, we face the dramatic power play between our unions and our districts resulting from required contract negotiations. These negotiations compel us to show our strength in numbers by walking on picket lines, attending rallies, leaving our children at home or carrying them on our backs as we rally at state capitals for more educational funding.

Meanwhile, we face words of derision in local and national media sources, which claim that our greed, not our passion, drives us. Contract negotiation time is abhorred by many of my most student-centered colleagues, as they require us to shift focus away from students and onto the needs of our institutions and to ensure that our livelihood isn't stripped from us. This cycle of contract negotiations, in combination with the regular emotional and spiritual requirements of the job, can easily lead to burnout for teachers who do not have in place a methodical solution for dealing with stress and emotional hardship.

Most teachers enter the profession armed with altruism and passion, but few are prepared for the strenuous emotional reality. Most graduate education programs do not provide courses in personal wellness or emotional health management. Few educate students about how the dynamics between unions and school districts create an emotional crevasse between teachers and their bosses. Many districts offer two to three year "probationary periods" in which newer teachers learn the craft and hone their skills before the district hires them permanently. The experience of being a probationary teacher during a contract negotiation year (which is going to happen to just about everyone since contract negotiations usually occur every two years) causes a distinct kind of stress. The newer teacher faces pressure to follow the district line if they wish to gain their permanent contract, yet the teacher also faces pressure from her fellow teachers to attend union actions in order to preserve class sizes, health care benefits, etc. This incredible stress, combined with the regular emotional requirements of the job makes it impossible to survive without a program of self-care.

Burnout Cycle

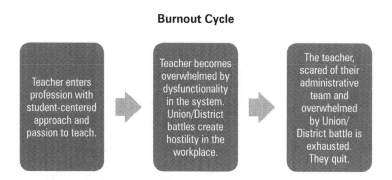

Teacher enters profession with student-centered approach and passion to teach.

Teacher becomes overwhelmed by dysfunctionality in the system. Union/District battles create hostility in the workplace.

The teacher, scared of their administrative team and overwhelmed by Union/District battle is exhausted. They quit.

Questions for Reflection:

If you were to create your own diagram about the burnout cycle, what would you add? What do you notice about people who leave the profession after several years of committed work?

1. What experiences in your career left you most overwhelmed? Can you describe an experience of being overwhelmed by anti-racist work?
2. How is being a teacher of color in the majority white school system a source of emotional stress?
3. How would you describe the most common stressors that come from being marginalized due to race? How does this impact your relationships with peers, students, and administrators?

Extremely tight schedules, short lunches, and few opportunities for students to meet with teachers during the school day require us to use every spare moment of the day to complete our work. Many of us use our 30-minute lunch break to meet with students, always staying after school for additional questions, and meeting with students during our prep period to ensure that all students have the resources and help that they need. When we are inside the system, facing the needs of 180 plus students, it is almost impossible, without withdrawing that integral emotional investment, to turn students away when they need us. For me, this means at least an hour of work each evening, plus at least three hours of work per weekend. As a young teacher without children, this level of commitment still seemed impossible, but it was doable. When I became a mother, I risked neglecting and ignoring my child to get my work done, unless I was willing to change my attitude and behavior toward work. The system must be transformed so that school schedules are humane for both teachers and students; until then, we must find ways to preserve our sanity within the dysfunction.

Motherhood saved my career by helping me to put into perspective the absolutely unrealistic expectations that I was placing on myself in response to the underfunding (and misdirection of funds) in U.S. public schools. I admit to muddling through the first two years of my daughter's life, fighting to commit every bit as much time to my work as I had before motherhood. In especially trying times, the feminist practice of deep-rooted self-love always reclaims her space in my life. She asks me to examine my right to be happy and free, just like I want for others. My inner feminist challenges me to reconsider how society is constraining or preventing me from being happy because of my gendered role (men also face gendered societal constraints). Her voice continually appeals to me as I see other mothers and fathers grappling with the fact that to excel, the system demands that we serve hundreds of students while sacrificing our relationship with our children. The work of battling the oppressive, racist nature of the system, while also experiencing the demoralizing aspects of the system can damage the spirit. My love for all children and my passion for the art of teaching continue to pull at me as well, causing this question to emerge from my consciousness: *How can we protect our individual dignity, mental, physical, emotional, and spiritual health within a system that requires us to face alienation, marginalization, and fatigue if we speak up against racism and work to transform it?* This transcendent question is pertinent for anyone who works in a capacity that requires them to face the antagonistic forces that go hand in hand with protesting and acting against the dominant system.

I answer by loving my body. I answer by caring for myself emotionally and spiritually. I bring my daughter into community and activism as much as possible. In doing so, being a role model for younger women and men who need to see examples of powerful adults who thrive within a school system that, undoubtedly, needs a complete transformation toward valuing educators and children. For me, care of my physical, emotional, and spiritual self must be part of my school day, so that when I am at home, I still have some capacity to give. When the schedule doesn't allow a break for me (or for the students who also rush through their day), I must carve out that break for all of us. When racism, sexism, gender normativity, and environmental pollution are not discussed in the mainstream curriculum, I must allow myself to inject them (or better yet build my whole curriculum around them). To survive, I must be an adult who pushes the institution to make space for real human beings. I must do so without apology. If attempts are made to correct or limit me, I allow myself to rebel. In this light, I must use the protection provided by my union contract to uphold my human needs—which include teaching for social justice. Employing me means that I get to be a human being with opinions, needs, and expectations of my own. I will do my best to live up to the expectations of my contract, but that does not mean I will allow myself to be abused by the system and it will, certainly, never silence me.

Questions for Reflection for Activist Teachers, Community Members, and Administrators:

Here are some questions to help you consider your emotional state as you work hard in the labyrinthine battle for educational equity:

1. On a scale of 1-10, how fatigued do I feel right now? How did I get here?
2. If I consider the episodes in this battle that make me feel fatigued, are they mostly related to occurrences inside the classroom, or with adults? If so, whom?
3. What emotional, spiritual, and physical practices do I have in place to cleanse myself throughout the inevitable drama of being an activist?
4. What words and ideas am I holding back? How does holding back my creative ideas that may be controversial harm me emotionally?
5. Who do I have in my school environment that can be a listener for me? Could I feel comfortable sharing these questions and answers with this person?

Strategies for Emotional Self-Care

As different students and situations come into my life each year, both breaking my heart and bringing me incredible joy, I also learn many lessons about myself. For me, hiring a professional counselor (who I see once every two weeks) is a requirement for my sanity. I am also engaged in a free program of recovery for people whose lives have been impacted by drug and alcohol abuse in family and friends, for which I attend a weekly meeting at night after my daughter is asleep. These resources have helped me to learn many tools for self-calming, communication, and ways to appropriately release anger through reflection and discussion. I would not have made it through numerous contract negotiations, student and staff deaths, or changes in my own life without utilizing these services that are readily available to me. Finding time to attend these sessions is difficult, but not more difficult than trying to make it in this profession without emotional support. I also use some specific techniques to create better emotional health during my school day. Here are a few:

Listening Partners

As an external processor, there are times when I just need to talk through a situation with a colleague who will listen. I have found a few amazing colleagues who are willing to be part of an exchange where we take turns just listening to one another's situations. We have a level of collegial respect that requires us to ask if the other person wants advice before we offer it. If the person doesn't want advice, it is perfectly ok for them to share with no questions asked, or remarks made. My favorite mental health strategy is when we can combine these listening sessions with a ten-minute walk on the track during part of lunch. This way, I can get some exercise, experience community, but get back to my students for the end of lunch to focus on their needs as well.

Here's a beneficial exercise to do with your listening partner: Sit together in a comfortable position. Set a timer for ten or twenty minutes. Lean your head back and say whatever word or phrase comes to mind. Allow for silence. Your partner takes a turn and does the same. This is not a conversation. Do not expect yourself to respond to what your partner said (unless that is what naturally comes out). Go back and forth trading phrases or words for the full ten or twenty minutes. This activity is a strategy for clearing out the mind and disposing of the unneeded words and ideas that can lead to confusion and overwhelm. Alternatively, it could be a good idea to go over the self-analysis questions about stress with a partner. Helping one another to recognize our stress is a strategy for self-care and community health.

Letter Writing

As I've grown as an educator, I've realized that voicing concerns that impact the classroom, cause teachers to leave the profession, and students to enter the school-to-prison pipeline is an intrinsic part of my life's work. At first, I was scared to blow the whistle; but now I see that many legislators desire relationships with excellent teachers, as many wish for money earmarked for schools to be used successfully. Through writing letters and building relationships, I have had several legislators visit my classroom; of those who have visited, all have invited me to keep in touch through email to communicate about nuances of the system that they may not see. In these communiqués, I *always* offer a viable solution to the problem I see. Legislators receive hundreds (sometimes thousands) of complaints. They would much rather read a viable solution from a seasoned educator, instead of a crazed rant from a dejected teacher who is an inch away from barricading herself into her classroom. If and when you write, always send a potential solution.

Maturing as a writer and educator has also helped me understand that shooting off a nasty email can reduce my ability to help to solve a problem. Last year, I promised myself to avoid sending angry emails whatsoever. When I think about the levels of mass incarceration and inequitable conditions in public schools, I see why many of us may be acting justly by showing our fury. Still, if you are inside the system, you are always measuring the potential outcomes of telling the truth. Can I get fired for calling this out? Will the union support me? Is free speech protected in the current manifestation of the United States? Sometimes I write the email, and then I click "save draft" instead of "send." Doing this allows me to vent without danger. The saved messages file can also be a useful way to record instances of injustice that you witness at your school. A series of saved emails can help to establish a pattern over time; just because you didn't send it today, that doesn't mean you won't send it in several months. Ultimately, more of us need to show our indignation, not hide it. Acting collectively, as teachers, community members, school employees, activists, and legislators will be crucial in inventing a just system of public education.

Spiritual Self-Care

If the passion to teach is honestly that—a passion, then it requires us to find that additional energy inside of ourselves to fuel our art. A poignant lesson, for me, comes from another place entirely. If students are to lose track of time, lose their grip on technology, and be inspired by what is happening in the classroom, I must find that inspiration within myself. Likewise, returning to the classroom after a student is shot or imprisoned, or speaking to students on the day before a potential strike (especially when I know how many first-generation college-bound students are counting on me to help with college applications, for example), requires a deep courage that, for me, can only come from beyond myself.

Spirituality is not a new concept in the field of social justice and education. The foundation of the 1950s Civil Rights Movement was the network of Black churches in the South. One cannot strip Christ away from the passionate speeches of Dr. King, nor can the singing of spirituals be divorced from the great marches. While keeping religion separate from the classroom is essential to public education; finding a spiritual source may aid you in surviving the system.

I cannot make suggestions about the ways others should embrace their spirituality. For clarity, I don't mean that we should all embrace some form of organized religion to find peace. Spirituality could be secular humanism, faith in nature, or hundreds of other possibilities. While I can't find what that is for anyone other than myself, here are some questions for consideration regarding how you might bring spirituality into your professional life in a way that will decrease the likelihood of burnout, and keep your motivation fresh:

1. How does my sense of spirituality connect with my motivation to teach or work as an activist?
2. What does my religion or spiritual practice teach with regard to equality and human dignity?
3. What does my spiritual practice teach about racism? How could I further align my practices with the aspect of my spiritual philosophy that rejects racism?
4. Where do I turn when I face a difficult challenge with a student, or even lose a student?

5. What private spiritual practice could I bring into my daily teaching practice that would help me to rejuvenate and better serve students?

Physical Self-Care

The physical aspects of activism and education are exceedingly challenging. Caring for the physical body is only recently becoming part of the culture of some work environments. Often, one must make a conscious decision to practice physical self-care, despite workplace policies that would otherwise harm the body.

Eating & Resting

Long-term activists and educators must find ways to ensure that we are eating healthy food and taking appropriate rest. Many activists tend toward a willingness to sacrifice ourselves to better society. Going without food or sleep to complete a task are common symptoms of this brand of self-sacrifice. To prevent burnout, we must feed ourselves, carry snacks, and provide ourselves with periodic breaks. Sometimes I just close my eyes and check in with myself to rate my level of tiredness. If I am exhausted, but must continue my work, I keep my eyes closed for an additional five to ten minutes before re-engaging in my project. These mini naps recharge my batteries. In them, I also express compassion and care towards myself—something I wish for others, and must find in myself if and when I can.

Movement

There are three forms of movement that I try to involve in each school day. Walking, Yoga, and Qi Gong help me to pause, reflect on my energy level, emotional and spiritual well-being and keep my blood and life energy moving. One of the best choices that I made early on in my career was to become certified to teach yoga. The yoga practice I developed taught me valuable lessons about breathing, emotions, and the way that energy moves through the body. I also learned how to identify feelings of emotional repression better—and to unbury them through movement.

There is a highly moralistic, largely white, culture of self-absorption and denial of other people's suffering disguised as self-healing and catharsis in the world of pay-to-play "yoga". Yoga has also become an indicator of white power and class privilege, especially visible here in Portland, where Saturday morning yoga and a smoothie are enjoyed by a certain class while the homeless population is expelled from a patch of woods just miles away. I'll be honest—I was very engaged in a yoga community. I even got my teaching certificate, but I saw the depth of that privilege in a conversation between wealthy whites at the teacher training that indicated some felt that their investment in yoga would bring them, spiritually, to a higher plane than those who do not practice yoga. This concept, and the evident class privilege (and designer sunglasses of those who made the comments), indicated the presence of a very dangerous classist and racist philosophy.

How do we bring mindfulness and movement into the classroom in a way that allows students to break free from the traditional classroom environment, while rejecting the culture of white supremacy and cultural appropriation around yoga and other Eastern movement and spiritual practices? For one, we must rebuild our entire system in a way that encourages free movement. We must admit that these Eastern practices (as well as forms of physical expression and dance that originate from Africa, Latin

America, and indigenous communities worldwide) can improve our current system, which is deeply entrenched with restrictive modalities of physical control originating from conservative movements in European religion and culture that dominate the very foundation of our public system's design. While we are still pushing up against that system, we must encourage the discussion of movement and appropriation while providing more opportunities for students to move freely in the classroom and around the school building. We must also create spaces where students are encouraged to express themselves physically in the way that they need to. In creating these spaces, we, as educators, will simultaneously create work environments that are more welcoming to communities of color and more humane for workers and students.

Punk Rock/Hip Hop/Art

The current system impacts educators by causing stress, fear, and anxiety. Working inside a system that perpetuates violence against those we serve hurts, especially when we realize that we are part of the clockwork. The resounding din of the school bells represents the institutionalization of young people, but also of teachers and school staff. Take the time to scream. Take the time to color outside of the lines. Punk Rock and Hip Hop are forms of cultural expression that originally emerged as responses to contexts of oppression. Inviting students to share their music, to write while listening to music, to research music, and to respond to literature by creating poetry, choreography, music, and art creates a classroom environment in which free expression and exploration are encouraged and celebrated. Students may even be able to release some of the stress that comes from various contexts of oppression that they face, whether these stressors are coming from the school environment itself, or the pressure of social class, racism, gender, or sexuality.

Movement in the Classroom

School environments restrict the movement of both teachers and students. After realizing the discomfort caused by small desks, designed and manufactured from the 1950s through the early 1980s, I scurried around to locate chairs and tables for my students. Though this makes a difference, it does not alter the restrictive schedules that students and teachers must follow, which also restrict free movement. Nor does it prevent students from staying seated. I now have a variety of movement activities and tools that I utilize to engage students. The activities and tools keep the blood flowing and release all of us from the idea of students as seated prisoners and the teacher as the master of the room. Incorporating movement is essential to a revolutionized pedagogy where students are empowered and encouraged toward full expression of their humanity

Meditation Balls and Hand Toys

Each summer, I pick up new sets of used meditation balls at Goodwill for about $1.99 each. I now have about 10 sets of meditation balls, several stress balls, several hand strengtheners that students can squeeze, ten mandala toys, and a few other items that students know they can pick up on their way in (and drop off on their way out). These items are *extremely helpful* for students who have trouble focusing. I find that almost all of the students like the idea, and most pick up a hand toy on their way in when they first learn about the concept. After a while, only the students who really need these items pick them up. I have never had one of these tools stolen or broken. The students show their appreciation for this alternative strategy by always returning them. I also allow students who forgot to pick one up at the start of class to come and get one at any time, which reduces fake bathroom breaks. I find that many students use the fake bathroom break just because they need to move their body. By giving students a way to move inside the classroom, the student is more likely to remain focused. A student standing up to take care of a physical need is not a nuisance; in my room, this is a good thing! The movement hand tools have been particularly beneficial, through my observations, with young people who have ADHD. I have seen this method incorporated into multiple Individualized Education Plans. I strongly encourage the collection of helpful hand toys that students can use to de-stress and focus their minds.

Throwing Games
After noticing how the students enjoyed the hand toys, I thought about the practices that are most commonly restricted in the classroom, especially those that young people seem to enjoy doing. I decided to purchase 15 soft balls to engage students in throwing and catching activities during class breaks. We started with the name game, where students stand in a circle and throw the ball to the next person, saying their name, and then we began adding balls; we had several flying around the room at once. Students enjoyed this as a group-building activity at the start of the year.

Then I realized the potential for this activity to be a vocabulary or question and answer strategy. For example, a student could ask a question about the text and pose that question to another student by throwing them the ball. That student cannot throw the ball forward without answering the question to the best of their ability. If they do not know the answer, they repeat the question and throw the ball to another student. If students are unable to answer, the ball holder throws the ball (and the question, figuratively) to the teacher—who knows that there is a collective need for an answer.

There are many ways to use the ball strategy. I understand how one might fear balls being thrown around the room, but I find that playing these games for five to ten minutes helps students refocus on their assignments. They tend to express gratitude simply for being able to stand up. Reflecting back on the culture of humiliation and control, allowing students to stand in their full height (and sometimes tower over me) is a huge trust builder. I am their short-fun-trusted teacher with the "lit" games. They are willing to listen to more complex philosophical concepts and take part in reading advanced material when I eliminate movement restriction, making the classroom more enjoyable.

Resting & Yogic Stretching

I also use uncomplicated yogic stretching in class. When I feel a lull, or when I notice that students are tired, I ask them to take a two to a three-minute respite. Sometimes I ask them to put their heads on their hands on their desks and rest. Then I ask them to stand up, shake out their hands and reach up above their heads. I ask them to reach for each elbow and gently stretch their side body. I ask them to engage in a few other moves that I gathered from yoga and Qi Gong. The surprising part is that they do it! If one person seems disinterested or taken aback, I let them know that I am not the yoga police. They laugh, and the majority use the time to move their bodies. The results are increased trust, reduced feelings of repression and control, and more laughter. This is also beneficial for me. Incorporating movement allows me to provide myself with that three to five-minute check-in so that I may give them my best.

Above all, finding an emotionally, spiritually, or physically grounding practice that you carry with you could help you to avoid burnout, as well as take action against racism. Without a spiritual foundation, facing such an endemic, often faceless beast can be too much to bear. As racist incidents go viral almost daily, an assaulting fatigue blankets many members of society. Students of color are often doubly exhausted by the expectation to be spokespeople in their classrooms about brutal racist videos that they have already seen dozens of times. For this reason, allowing the classroom to be a refuge where students feel welcome and comfortable, is critical to maintaining the mental health of both ourselves and our students.

PART III

Total Transformation: Structural Change for Victory over Racism

C onnecting with students beyond the surface level is a crucial aspect of excellent pedagogy, but excellent teaching must be accompanied by the major transformation of the entire system if we are to eradicate the racist, classist principles that govern the underlying structure of the current system.

We must examine the ways that our district offices, administrators, unions, and parent-teacher organizations unconsciously perpetuate racism. This section carefully examines each of these categories, offering suggestions for radically renovated structures that will drive our whole system toward actualizing the dream of fully serving, challenging, and including all young people.

There is no quick-fix to the nationwide reality of racism in public education. There are changes that teachers can make to their pedagogical style within their classrooms to create greater equity within a corrupt and dysfunctional system, and then there is the revolution that must take place if public education is ever to escape from historical patterns of dysfunction and equitably serve the whole populous. The

A DIFFERENT VISION

revolution will require extensive changes in almost every aspect of operation and infrastructure. To focus this discussion on a quasi-realistic set of changes that could be made with the right determination and collective community of educators, let's examine potential changes in the areas of educational administration, unions, funding, community relationships, school building design and scheduling, and the role of social work in education.

In sharing my utopian model for equitable schools, I ask for criticism and afford myself (and YOU) the opportunity to truly think creatively about how we, as a nation, can move forward, through all of the obstacles, toward a better system. While I write with a more critical tone in this section, please do not mistake it for hopelessness. Social criticism is perhaps one of the highest forms of hope. I cannot apologize for my somber analysis; it is required to uncover the vision for the future. I premise this theoretical imagining on two distinct beliefs: 1) While technology will play a greater role in education, humans still thrive best when they are physically present and engaged with one another. 2) The human need for interaction, role modeling, and engagement with older adults (both older children, parents, and teachers) will never make the role of the teacher or mentor obsolete. Beyond these two basics, my creative vision considers, as much as possible, obstacles that we will face in efforts to transform our system entirely. The editorial process is, perhaps, the most sacred tool of the collective envisioning process. By interacting with this text, can we, together, envision a viable plan? The next few parts of this text examine a problem, offer a creative set of solutions, and then propose a set of discussion questions that you can discuss with yourself, a peer, or in a classroom, or living room setting.

7

Educational Administration & A Model for Teacher Leadership

Castles Made of Sand: Administrative Leadership Model Built to Destroy

In 2003, at the age of 23, when I entered Franklin High School as a brand new teacher, the school was in poor shape. The graduation rate was dismal—around 60% for some subgroups. Literacy tests came back with "poor" scores. The school had a reputation in the community for being a place where teachers came to work for their last few years before retirement. Dr. Charles Hopson, a Black principal who acutely saw the inequities in the school, hired me. Dr. Hopson was on a mission to change Franklin's trajectory. He worked hard to encourage retirement of a few educators who were occupying their classrooms, but sincerely no longer teaching. He also brought the issue of racial inequity to the forefront of the administrative agenda. Before he left to pursue a superintendent position in another district, he asked me to work with the district grant writer to apply for the multi-million dollar SLC-PREP grant, which we won.

A DIFFERENT VISION

Fortunately, when he departed, Shay James, a Black woman who he mentored, stepped up to become the principal. The Advanced Scholar Program, which I founded in 2007 with a small group of fellow teachers, was recognized by the National Education Association, the Oregon Education Association, and the College Board for dramatically increasing the number of students of color taking AP and Dual Credit courses and heading to college. When SLC-PREP funds ran dry, Nike School Innovation Fund offered financial support. The school district also decided to fund the program in their general budget with $50,000 per year. Through collaboration between teachers, counselors, and this excellent activist administrator and her team, the entire school culture shifted from a culture of failure to a college-going culture. Our eight AP courses grew to 18. Since 2008, the overall graduation rate increased by nearly 10%. During the period in which Principal James shared the reins of power with her staff, we faced the collapse of another struggling school community into our own—nearly doubling the size of the school and increasing the population of students (which was already above 50%) living in poverty by more than ten percent. Despite tremendous obstacles, we continued to succeed, bringing our graduation rate within one point of the wealthiest public school in the district. In the five years between 2011 and 2016, I had seven Gates Scholars in my senior AP English course, graduating along with hundreds of other scholarship winners who were supported by an incredible community of educators. Let me clarify the level at which these administrators, especially Principal James and then Vice Principal Ivonne Dibblee, operated. In addition to focusing on hiring teachers of color, challenging educators with antiquated racist practices, and supporting a culture of excellence, they also kept a secret list of students who needed a free ticket to prom due to poverty. They worked with the teaching staff, including me, to identify the students who needed an increased variety of supports—and personally reached out their own hands to ensure both systemic and personal support.

This focus on equity earned me a National Education Association Award and the OnPoint Award for Excellence in Education (an awesome award that paid my mortgage for a year!). Principal James was tapped to move up to a position of district leadership, senior director of high schools. She took the position, leaving the leadership of Franklin High School open. While I believe that she tried to communicate about the nuanced manner in which she shared power with staff, really involving us in decision making, some of the administrative successors did not adopt a radical teacher-leadership model. I found myself floundering to maintain the excellent program that I created with my colleagues—unable to lead in the way I had before based on continuous roadblocks from the new administration. Just like that, a change in leadership brought the dream of a shared-leadership model to an end. The new administration made the decision to authorize a sports literature class at the 11th grade level, which was originally proposed as a way to engage boys of color (a bizarre move considering the fact that we had the highest graduation rate for boys of color in the state in the years when they were intentionally encouraged toward college-credit bearing courses). Sickened by the racism in this decision, which countered the philosophy of challenging all students toward collegiate success through opportunities for advancement, I could no longer lead in the capacity I had before. I decided to depart. To save myself as a teacher, I had to depart from my title and my legacy of outstanding success to continue my equity work at another school. In the same year, several other teachers departed. I felt that the administration could not tolerate the idea that teachers shared power. The future of the school is unknown; although, according to the 2017 State Report Card, writing test scores and success of priority students (traditionally marginalized students) have already declined. Though experiencing this was extremely painful, as it involved the loss of a dream, it is not at all uncommon. A colossal challenge facing public education is the routine shifts in leadership that topple the excellent work of teachers and school staff for the sake of maintaining hierarchical control. Thriving school programs wash away like sand castles in the crashing waves of power-hungry administrators who wish to lay their claim on schools and then depart—leaving both the children and the teachers behind. School programs that focus on innovative approaches to solving inequity are at the greatest risk, as their continuation relies on the values and belief system of the new administrator. Since such a small percentage of school administrators are people of color, the likelihood of finding a replacement principal who will automatically fund and support equity initiatives is small. This reality exacerbates the distrust communities of colors have towards schools. Parents have to guess when schools are heading for disaster, or worse, they must send their children regardless of the deficiency of the leadership structure, while wealthy whites, en masse, have the choice to pluck their children out and send them to private school.

In a *Washington Post* article, writer Valerie Strauss reports that a 2012 Rand Corporation study showed that 20% of principals leave the post within one to two years.

In my own experience, if a vice principal stays longer than three or four years, they soon begin to itch for a principal position. Likewise, a principal who stays longer than five years expects to move to the mysterious labyrinth of the district office (the land of $100,000+ salaries). The research shows what common sense already illustrates—quickly disappearing leaders lead to a pattern of discarded initiatives, poor relationships between teachers and administrators, and failing schools. Unsurprisingly, struggling schools, often populated by higher rates of students of color and students living in poverty, face higher rates of shifting leadership. The Hechinger Report documents that 30% of principals who lead struggling schools quit every year. By year three, the report states, more than half of principals leave their positions. The answer, however, is not principals who stay longer, holding top-down authority over schools for extended periods of time.

Along with being ineffective due to these constant changes, the hierarchical structure of school administration is one that is rooted in patriarchy and white supremacy. According to the AFL-CIO's Department of Professional Employees, in 2013, 13.4 percent of education administrators were Black or African American, 2.6 percent were Asian, and 5.8 percent were Hispanic or Latino. Native American administrators made up such a small number that they were not listed in the statistics. All told, this equates to 21.8% administrators of color in a system with more than 50% students of color. Beyond these abysmal statistics on representation is the reality that the administrative hierarchy itself comes from a Eurocentric model, nested in a hunger for power and control over a subservient workforce that then renders the students as the lowest members of the hierarchy.

The very concept of the solitary leader (almost always white and male until the mid-1980s) who has the final say is antithetical to the idea of a collective vision that operates in many communities of color. Governance by a supreme individual who delegates authority to lower-level administrators to enforce policy through teachers is so clearly demonstrative of an archaic, sexist, tyrannical leadership model. Furthermore, what does this model teach students about individual empowerment, critical thinking, questioning authority, and systems analysis for greater efficiency? Instead of role modeling cooperation and the power of collective vision and action, this spirit-crushing model requires students to *disassociate* from the idea that they could be empowered to make important decisions in their school community. This disassociation at the school level is the first step toward disengagement from the political process and feelings of inefficacy toward authority.

Sadly, within the system, the principal is the person who is ultimately responsible for issuing suspensions or expulsions, which are handed down to students of color at exceedingly high rates. A student of color facing the final judgment of the administrator, who acts as a conduit for the inherent supremacy of the system, can only feel a great distrust for both the individual and the system. We must abolish this hierarchical model of school leadership and replace it with a collective and community-based leadership model with student input if we are to work toward eradicating the school-to-prison pipeline.

In speaking for the abolition of the entire structure of school leadership in the United States, I almost want to apologize to the few excellent principals and vice principals I know who make every effort to operate justly in a corrupt system. However, I believe most of them would agree that the current system is not operating effectively, except as a source of oppression for communities of color and a source of social and academic promotion for white students. Current administrators who give their entire lives to schools, often struggling with their district offices in ongoing wars to allocate funding to their specific schools, know that the system is broken. There are also countless school leaders who do understand the importance of teacher and student empowerment as opposed to hierarchical leadership, yet (even if they activate forms of student and teacher leadership in their communities) they still accept their role in the hierarchical model and take pay for it. The reinvention of the system in a way that benefits communities of color will require total removal of the opportunity to profit through hierarchical forms of control.

As previously discussed, a metamorphosis toward student empowerment must take place at the classroom level to weed out humiliation, alienation, and power-tripping. These same dynamics, perpetuated by the administrative structures in schools, breeds resentment and distrust in both students and staff. The long-term benefits of the traditional model of school leadership in the United States, are, apparently, only that they hold the status quo—upholding the structure of white supremacy, feeding the prison system, and withholding great creativity of teachers and students alike.

Berry, Byrd, and Wieder in their book *Teacherpreneurs: Innovative Teachers Who Lead But Don't Leave,* explore teacher leadership in U.S. schools. Reading this text, and experiencing the challenges of being a teacher leader in a hierarchical system, helped to solidify my belief that we must empower the humble, long-term educators who already struggle, over decades, to operate and maintain programs that are under constant threat from changing administrators, many who want to make their mark and depart. The book, which I highly recommend, offers examples of teachers in leadership roles in unique schools throughout the country. While some forward-thinking schools are offering teacher-leadership opportunities, a revolution in the management of schools is not yet taking place, nor are existing teacher leadership positions always created with the intention of eradicating racism.

How could schools operate without administrators and collective leadership for greater equity? How can we take the supremacy out of school administration—service, teaching, rotation of leadership? How do we envision a new model for schools when we are products of institutionalization?

I recently met a principal who had over 35 years in public education, with more than 15 as a vice principal (of course at a variety of schools). While this individual has a great deal of experience, that experience comes from a corrupt, racist system. Institutions, after long periods of time, leave imprints on people; just like ex-convicts who struggle with the lack of structure in life on the outside, principals may become entrenched in the hierarchy and even corrupted by their institutional power; they may struggle to open themselves to new concepts like teacher leadership.

Moreover, principals and district leaders who spend many years in a system that is rooted in nepotism, corruption, miscommunication, and misallocation of funds, at best, will operate with a scarcity mindset. So many years of scrounging for resources, making due with less, and expecting teachers and students to deal with abhorrent conditions does not manifest an environment for creative brainstorming and change. A new generation of parents, teachers, and community members must unite to deconstruct the current system to wholly eradicate the corruption in the current system and the scarcity mindset that it engenders.

A Model for Teacher Leadership

To finally dismiss the culture of white supremacy in schools, we must do away with the top-down approach to school administration. This dismissal will entail total deconstruction of the hierarchical model of school administration. There are many models of democratic, teacher-led programs currently employed in small schools, usually private or magnet, globally. There are few if any, entire districts in the United States that have eradicated educational administrators and authorized a community and teacher leadership model. It may seem strange and impossible to consider comprehensive public high school operating without principals and vice principals. Suggesting the complete eradication of the current hierarchical model may seem to teeter on the ridiculous side of radical, but any authentic educator knows that to get to viable solutions, we must sometimes clear the table of all assumptions to discover a genuinely effective solution. Perhaps the current system is so planted in the roots of U.S. public schools that it would be impossible to implement change at a large scale level, but it could also be true that envisioning how schools could operate with a collectivist process could bring us one step closer to the goal of equitable schools. Please open your mind to this different vision for how that could take place. There will be an opportunity to question and critique this hypothetical model.

The Teacher Leaders and Community Member Administrative Model

Teacher leaders and community members take on the roles associated with principals and vice principals for limited terms, elected by the school community, parents, and fellow teachers. Roles include: teacher leader for equity and data analysis, teacher leader for budget and accounting, teacher leader for school climate and community, teacher leader for curriculum and instruction, teacher leader for athletics, teacher leader for the arts, teacher leader for special education, teacher leader for acceleration, teacher leader for mental health, etc. These teachers are paid at the same rate as their fellow teachers, but teach no more than half-time so that they may dedicate the rest of their time to systems analysis, direct service to students, and community engagement. If additional nighttime work is required for any of these positions, these teachers are paid at their hourly rate for a limited number of hours per quarter that must be documented. Additionally, these teacher leaders are required to work an additional three to four weeks during the summer and are compensated for their time in accordance with union guidelines.

The same roles that exist for teachers exist for community members. In other words, there is both a teacher leader for equity and data analysis and a community leader for equity and data analysis and so on and so forth. The community leader, probably a parent or alum, works with the school leader to operate the school through consensus, and student and community input through regular surveys. The community leader is paid at an hourly rate for a designated number of hours not to exceed a set amount per quarter.

This administrative model requires the representation from diverse groups within its board of teachers and community leaders. A balancing limitation dictates that the board of teacher and community leaders membership does not exceed 50% white (the school community can alter these limitations depending on the ethnic and racial breakdown of the school itself). All teacher and community leaders take a vow of service and are sworn into their positions. If they need to resign or take a leave of absence for any reason (pregnancy, etc.) first and second runners-up act as alternates, unless the equity balance will be thrown off, in which case the runner-up serves as a substitute while an impromptu election occurs.

Note to current administrators: This model does not negate the need for skilled educational leaders who are prepared to serve their communities; in fact, it would make it easier for outstanding leaders to both find their focus and obtain leadership positions. If you are an equity-focused principal who loves your job, can you see how this system would eradicate the needs for constant battles between unions and districts that overshadow the focus on equity? Instead of seeing yourself in the role of ruler, this model allows you to view your position as a community leader, who is on equal footing, along with all of the other individuals in the community.

This negation of the current role of educational administrators may seem surprising and insulting. But why? Our system is currently unsuccessful. Corruption in district hierarchies is rampant. Distrust between teachers and administrators is the bread and butter of the system. This model does not entirely remove roles for those individuals who have vision and talent as logistical operators or visionaries; it suggests that these positions are in no way more significant than teachers and other staff. It also suggests that no one who is not in part working with students should be making decisions for those of us who do. Could this vision that I suggest be improved, perhaps by current administrators who would see some flaws? Perhaps. Likewise, schools will improve when current educators make decisions about how schools operate in communion with other teachers, community members, and students.

Some may be wondering if I am suggesting that current administrators be removed from their posts and given salary cuts to the level of a teacher. Yes. Exactly that—though my vision does propose that teachers who take on supplementary leadership roles be compensated for their additional time, including pay for their summer work. If current teachers at the top of their pay scale earn about $70,000, teachers in leadership roles may earn $10,000 to $15,000 more given their summer work.

The exact details of the teacher leadership model and associated compensation package will have to be worked at extensively. The goal is to remove the hierarchical model and turn to a community-based leadership model. Doing so may help to increase the numbers of people of color in leadership roles, bring parents of color into leadership positions, and make our schools feel less like a frightening, white institution, and more like a rich learning community with diverse and inclusive leadership.

Questions for Reflection:

1. What other roles could be completed by teacher and community leaders?

2. What is missing from this picture? If teachers and parents were the leaders in your school community, what roles would they play?
3. Who would you nominate for leadership positions? What are the flaws in the teacher leadership model that I propose? What should be added?

Data Clerks & Administrative Assistants

Data clerks and administrative assistants play a crucial role in keeping schools focused on equity. Administrative assistants and data clerks operate the main office and complete work and data analysis as needed by each teacher and community leader. Monthly grade and attendance reports, for example, would be examined by the teacher leader for equity and their team. Data is used to drive instruction and understand inequities in the school environment. If one teacher repeatedly fails male students of color, instead of targeting the boys of color as individual trouble-makers, the equity team calls for a review of the teacher's instructional practices, offering assistance as a remedy. This process eradicates the thin blue line that currently exists—teachers protecting teachers who have racist or sexist views. Through technology, regular tracking, and a more objective and equity-centered approach, we can move toward a system that confronts racism rather than hiding it under bundles of unexamined papers and white supremacist attitudes. Data clerks are also used to track teachers entering and leaving work, as well as taking sick days, personal days, etc. Data clerks carry the responsibility for accountability concerns that come up, as well as administrative tasks related to extended pay, etc. Each school is provided with a data clerk at the rate of 1 per 300 students.

system than the success of black and brown children. White adults who currently work as counselors and have professional degrees in counseling and social work must be able to see their supremacy. As whites, we all must admit that we can't say that we do anti-racist work while accepting the benefits of white supremacy and excluding minorities from interacting with the children of their specific communities.

In a seven-period day, all teachers teach five classes per day plus one class period called *Teacher as Social Worker*. Teacher as Social Worker is a time allotted for performing the social work aspect of the job, which requires a specified number of parent phone calls per month, as well as a specified number of in-person student tutoring session per month. These must be documented and turned in to the data clerks. Since we know that human beings operate best with intrinsic and extrinsic rewards, teachers who go above and beyond in parent contact will be publically acknowledged. A seventh period is for prep time and committee work once per week. Once per week, each teacher meets with the teacher leader of their team (equity team, special education team, budget team, etc.). Community and student leaders attend these meetings once per month; Google Hangouts or other forms of technology are an acceptable vehicle for a meeting if the parent cannot physically attend.

Alternative Options for Educational Administration

The process of radical creative envisioning can help us to find the elements of teacher leadership that we can blend into the current system. I placed my creative vision for complete teacher leadership ahead of a vision for partial teacher leadership for three main reasons: 1) The current system is not functioning on behalf of all students, and we must look

Other Aspects of the Teacher Leadership Model

School counselors are hired at the rate of 1 per 75 studer
Counselors also teach college and career classes to th
caseload of students as part of the schedule, so that th
see each student regularly. But this is not enough. Schoo
must analyze the language and culture needs of all studei
in the community and use this data in the counselor hiri
process. The overwhelming majority of school counsel(
in the United States are white females. They do not have t
skills needed to address the needs of our growing Lati
African American, Middle Eastern, and Asian communit
They often cannot communicate well with parents or t
students themselves. Stringent certification requireme
must include more leeway so that language and cultu
proficiency can be used to fulfill some requirements of t
license. For example, if a potential counselor does not m
every requirement, but meets most, they must be allowec
gain certification through subbing in their language and
cultural ability for one or two of the requirements they
not, by state standards, meet. All counselors must have
understanding of child or adolescent psychology, trau
sexual abuse, the impact of drug addiction on homes a
families, and community resources, but people can g
and document these skills in various ways. The fact that
current system mandates collegiate training in all of th
areas, but allows whites to dominate school counseling
an abhorrent example of white supremacy. That the syst
trains and promotes middle class whites as intermediai
to black and brown homes rather than including black a
brown adults as counselors shows that maintaining
social class position of white adults is more important to

to creative, original, and unorthodox ideas to begin the shift needed to rectify the problem. 2) I would rather experience the criticism that my ideas are too radical as opposed to status quo. 3) Given my experiences as an educator, I have more faith in the ability of teachers to operate schools than I do in transient administrators who enter schools via a system of domination that trickles down to every aspect of student's lives; sadly, trickle-down economics is incredibly ineffective when it comes to equitable education.

While we must consider the possibility of educational administration continuing to be a career path, what aspects of teacher leadership do we wish to preserve and support within the current hierarchical paradigm? Which aspects do we wish to discard? The following principles could guide administrators toward increased effectiveness in schools:

- *Educational administrators must see themselves as public servants who are present to assist professional educators in serving schools.*

- *The educational administration must work against top-down, hierarchical management styles through promoting teacher leadership—and avoiding token teacher leadership.*

- *Districts must provide budgets for teacher leadership so that principals may release teachers from full teaching loads and support their leadership roles.*

- *Teacher leaders can be employed in positions currently operated by educational administrators to create improved school environments, meaning eradicating unnecessary educational administration positions to support more teacher leadership.*

- *Teacher leaders must be supported through release time (half day teaching, half leadership position) to operate healthy school restorative justice, attendance, and academic and college readiness programs. Some version of this model could function within the current structure that includes educational administrators to achieve more successful schools.*

- *Unions must support teacher leadership roles and encourage variations in teaching schedules in ways that lead to more opportunities for teacher empowerment.*

- *Teacher leadership roles must operate based on a rotation of leadership; teacher leaders must experience feedback from fellow teachers; teacher leadership could operate on a term basis, so other teachers have the opportunity to work in these positions.*

How, though, is teacher leadership related to creating more equitable teaching environments? Teachers work regularly with students for a good part of the day and experience the reality of teaching. As such, they possess a greater sense of empathy and sharper knowledge about needs of the students, teachers, and school environment. *Being in touch* is often missing in educational administration. Often, well-meaning administrators are forced to operate with a sense of triage regarding the needs of students, teachers, and school buildings. This selective listening means that schools become dysfunctional. When one teacher's need for AP Environmental Science books falls by the wayside because administrators decided that another school need is more important, that teacher loses faith in the system, and her students are underserved due to the gross negligence that is part of the current fabric of educational administration and funding. Equity, then, becomes an afterthought, lost in the battle to shout the loudest about one's unaddressed classroom needs. Teachers know this dynamic and understand the pitfalls of hierarchical systems that ignore the needs of the multitudes to support the next popular initiative. Teachers are more likely to exhibit compassion toward fellow teachers and students—and address the issues hindering the creation of a proper system of administration. Can a skillful principal do this? Quite possibly, but not without teacher leadership.

Exceptional teacher leadership will invite collective vision into the planning and governance process of public schools. To extract white supremacy from public education is to move away from hierarchical leadership styles founded in white supremacy. The Eurocentric hierarchical model, closely linked to the patriarchal family model, must be abolished if we are to move forward to a more positive organizational psychology that invites in the perspective, leadership styles, needs, and voices of the entire community. Attempts to reform the current system that rely on the hierarchical model will never successfully oust institutional racism. Children in this system will continue to learn that they are the least powerful; teachers will continue to harbor resentment against their leaders; leaders will continue to reap the financial benefits of corruption while making only marginal changes, or continuing the cycle that harms Black, Latino, and Native American children the most. Total system transformation requires disassembly of the very architecture of white supremacy. If no resolution is found to curb the systemic barriers that feed the school-to-prison pipeline, we must demand revolution.

A revolutionized public education system has numerous benefits. Within this revolutionized system hierarchy is replaced with collaborative community-operated schools. Schools are staffed by more adults who better represent the students they serve, leading to less disciplinary problems, greater feelings of connectedness between students and school staff, restored community between school staff and the community, and students who are viewed as (and see themselves as) potential community leaders. This model, or one like it, could dismantle the ongoing battle for power between unions and educational administrators, putting the onus of public education into the hands of educators (no longer divided) and community members. Letting go of the battle for power will offer us the opportunity to reinvent public education, inviting in long-withheld perspectives of communities of color to finally achieve greater equity in our schools.

8

The Union of Values

Mr. Smith doesn't teach—he just hands out work-sheets and grades us based on how many we are turning in! Mr. Smith just puts on movies! Mr. Smith is so unfair—he accused me of not turning in my work, but I took a picture of myself putting it in his box, and he still didn't give me credit even though he lost it! Mr. Smith is racist—he always kicks the Black girls out because he says we are loud—but he chums it up with the white football guys! It is so unfair. During the early years of my teaching career, I regularly heard the complaints about a teacher who shall go by Mr. Smith, and I know that school community members reported their complaints to the administration, but nothing ever happened to him. In fact, when certain coaching positions opened up, Mr. Smith seemed to get the job before it was posted on the district website. His position as a pillar of the school community was so solid that he seemed untouchable.

In my interactions with Mr. Smith, as a young white female teacher, I noticed that he was extremely dismissive, if not rude—he seemed to be relying on the concept of the older white male patriarch/coach as a gift to the teaching community. I began to read his dismissiveness and his arrogance as a mask he wore to maintain a sense of superiority in the community, so he could go on doing very little under

174 **A DIFFERENT VISION**

the guise of upholding a standard of excellence and defining the school's posterity. But when I heard from a young Mexican American female that he had said, during class, it was best never to marry a Mexican woman because they are pretty when they are young, but get fat when they are older; I was outraged. I began to ask questions about why he was allowed to continue to teach.

When I spoke to the administrator, asking questions about this scenario, he told me he could not release the details of the situation. However, I had a close relationship with the administrator. He told me that this was the tip of the iceberg. He told me that there were many similar occurrences. The best he could do was document, utilize the contractual requirement to place struggling teachers on a plan of assistance, and hope for support from his higher-ups at the district in combating the union, which was aligned with educators who made egregious errors in dealing with students, often demonstrating gender or race-based bias. He challenged me to confront my union and ask why they supported these teachers when multitudes of students and parents had written formal complaints over several years. The administrator highlighted that the situations he referred to were not circumstances where a teacher had one solitary complaint and needed union support during an investigation. These were situations where teachers had dozens of complaints on file, yet they were still allowed to collect their salary, and eventually to retire with publically funded retirement plans.

When I began being more vocal in staff meetings or in one-on-one conversations about bias in the teaching staff, I became a pariah in the teacher lounge. They stole my lunch from the teacher's lounge fridge, which was behind a door that only teachers had the key to. One older teacher approached me, saying, "Stop messing with the veteran teachers." They let me know they hated me through mean glances, hateful expressions, whispers, and lies. They offered me the same treatment they gave to children who did not meet their standards or behave in a docile manner during their flat, lackluster lectures. I was young and felt trapped in this isolating dynamic; I often cried alone. Fortunately, my education in the history of social movements told me that my sadness about being ostracized by some of my colleagues could never compare to the barking dogs and fire hoses pointed at protestors during the Civil Rights Movement (or the torture that the student of Mexican heritage was subjected to by Mr. Smith). I kept those images in my mind as I searched the school staff for allies who saw what I saw.

Luckily, I befriended a school security officer who more than understood the reality that I observed. He was the person called to certain classrooms to remove African American and Latino students who were being ejected from class by white teachers who were not culturally competent. He was the miracle worker who helped salvage the little bits of self-esteem that remained in these marginalized students, year after year. We began to eat lunch together in my room. Together, we discussed the teachers who we felt understood the dynamics but were silent due to fear. He helped me to get through those early years, encouraging me to build alliances with those who were like-minded. Meanwhile, the administration began hiring more staff of color—who I worked hard to befriend when they came into the school. Over thirteen years, we built alliances and shifted the school culture to create a better place for our students of color (described in detail in the appendix). However, even after the school won national, state, and local awards for excellence in educational equity (despite carrying along some teachers who staunchly opposed the changes we made to achieve greater equity), the teachers who received annual complaints regarding racist practices continued to experience support from the union. All of them remained employed until retirement. Many are still teaching; the rest are collecting on nice retirement packages.

I do not wish to unequivocally validate the common narrative that unions protect bad teachers, as I know hundreds of excellent teachers who I am glad to call colleagues. Unions are one of the last sacred institutions that safeguard schools. They fight for reasonable class sizes, fair pay for highly qualified and professional educators, and defense against administrative bullying or incompetence. But a system of "due process" that does not examine the potential bias of employees or screen for multiple complaints of bias over time needs some reconsideration. Teachers unions, comprised largely of white teachers, do contain members with sexist, racist, classist, and homophobic attitudes. We, as union members and as a community, must view the eradication of sexism, racism, classism, and anti-LGBTQ rhetoric in our unions as means of strengthening our collective power. Teachers unions will be much stronger if we affirm that we do not accept racist, sexist, or anti-LGBTQ behavior or attitudes. Bigoted attitudes, especially when there are multiple complaints, which, negates the possibility of a misunderstanding, must not be protected in any way if we are to claim to be oriented toward social and racial justice.

The Paradox of Union Loyalty

Much has been written about the problems facing teachers unions. In his article, *Teachers Unions and the War Within*, Mike Antonucci writes, "The teachers unions now face an environment in which their traditional enemies are emboldened, their traditional allies are deserting, and some of their most devoted activists are questioning the leadership of their own officers." This statement relates to the disorganization, corruption, and errors in leadership facing many teachers unions in the United States; in fairness, the statement also reflects the impact of constant attacks on organized labor by the conservative machine, and specific attacks on teachers unions by state and federal power-mongers.

As a dedicated member of the Portland Association of Teachers, I see how union leadership relentlessly wars with our school district to protect teachers. When I faced a situation with a violent student, my union protected me. When administrators bullied me, my union protected me. When workplace issues hampered my ability to teach, my union was there for me. When I witnessed a young teacher of color being harassed by an administrator, my union and I were there to surround him with support. When the union fights, I fight. Still, I see the ways that union politics (and similar organizations across the nation) negatively impact students of color by keeping the focus on key economic concerns. Like any organization, their primary focus is to serve their constituents. In as much as our union can protect the needs of students—like through fighting for smaller class sizes, livable working conditions, and state funding for education as a whole—they do. But the needs of students do not come first; rather, the union fights for the needs of the students when those needs overlap with what teachers need to be successful in the classroom and viable economically. Often, these needs do coalesce; however, it should be no surprise that most unions do not make racial justice for students their main priority. We, the 82%, are protectors of the status quo of racism in public schools due to how we place our needs for "fair labor practices" before the need to eradicate racism in public education. When Portland teachers go out to the Broadway Bridge to protest, we are protesting about large class sizes, unfair wages, attempts to take away our benefits and attempts to break down our bargaining power. But when the Black Lives Matter Movement clashed with the police after taking over the local mall, the teachers union was not present. Ending exclusionary discipline, removing barriers to advanced coursework for Black, Latino, or Native American students, or eradicating other forms of institutionalized racism aren't at the forefront of any public materials or contract negotiations either. While the leadership of two recent Portland Association of Teachers created a concept of unionism grounded in the principles of social justice, it remains true that the final battles regarding the contract are related to labor rights and quality of service to the student population, not specifically focused on racial equity.

Logically, unions in places with higher concentrations of Black, Latino, and Native American youth would reflect a specific focus on the needs of these populations; however, this is not the case. Due to the over-arching attack on public education, educators are forced to focus on protecting their professional benefits, compensation packages, and maybe building conditions and class sizes (issues that also impact the public health of students). And we know that even in areas with high populations of African American, Latino, and Native American students, teaching populations continue to be majority white.

The tightly woven thread of Puritanical American values constructs the ideological fabric of unions. The ideas that, hard works pays off, altruistic service is invaluable, and teaching is a sublime profession that society must support through public funding guide social justice unionism. These are some of the core concepts that fire teachers up as they protest each year in state capitols or outside of their school district offices. What really happens, however, is that public education in the United States does not serve communities of color in the same manner as white students. Public education does not protect the fabric of democracy—it feeds Black, Latino, and Native American children into the school-to-prison, while safeguarding white children so that *they* may participate in "democracy." This conflict, then, results from a total disconnect between the ideology of unionism and the reality of public education in the United States. While this may not be the intention of the teachers, many of whom fight for, feed, and love students from the above groups; the failure of our unions to crusade against racism—as our primary issue—permits the continuation of systemic barriers to civil rights.

Questions for Reflection:

1. What are the priorities in your union or the union that represents your children's teachers? If you are a parent or administrator, you can examine the union website to explore the key issues that they are focusing on.

2. Is racial justice mentioned in the list of key demands the union is currently making? What language, if any, is used to describe racial inequality?

3. Does the union accept any role or responsibility in the battle for racial equality in schools?

4. Does the union use specific language to hold the district accountable for working toward racial equity in schools? What is being said regarding the role of professional educators in the battle against racism in public education?

5. Does your union or the union representing your children's teachers regularly support teachers who have received numerous complaints of racist practices? Which representative in your union would be best to ask about this particular issue?

CHALLENGE FOR PARENTS, ADMINISTRATORS, TEACHERS, AND SCHOOL STAFF:

Write emails, letters, and call your local union leadership to request an end to defending educators who have multiple complaints of racist practices. Relentlessly call and email until your voices are heard!

The Exclusionary Ethos of Radical Unionism

In his article, *A Revitalized Teacher Union Movement,* former President of the Milwaukie Teacher's Education Association, Bob Peterson artfully describes the attack on teachers unions by the Koch Brothers and their movement against organized labor and public education. He also addresses, in part, the reality that most teachers unions are not solely focused on social justice. He does so by introducing the following principles of social justice unionism, which he states are not often utilized as guiding principles:

"Three components of social justice unionism are like the legs of a stool. Unions need all three to be balanced and strong:

- We organize around bread and butter issues.
- We organize around teaching and learning issues to reclaim our profession and our classrooms.
- We organize for social justice in our community and in our curriculum."

Peterson goes on to suggest that unions can be sources of professional development, citing the following tenets:

"Our teaching and learning work has focused on reclaiming our profession in three primary ways:

1. We provide professional development and services to our members.
2. We advocate/organize around specific demands to reclaim our classrooms and our profession.
3. We partner with the MPS administration through labor/management committees to ensure maximum success of district initiatives and practices."

He discusses the union's role in anti-racist civil rights work, citing a workshop where union participants read passages from Lisa Delpit's *Multiplication is for White People.* Peterson should be applauded for his exemplary leadership against corporate giants, and for his wise movement toward a revitalized model of unionism that places social justice at the center of union activism.

The Principles of Anti-Racist Unionism

While Peterson deserves applause for his work to describe a model for social-justice oriented unionism, readers must note that even in, arguably, the most well-organized, radical, and active teachers union in the nation, the *primary focus* is not ending apartheid-like policies that feed the school-to-prison pipeline. This critique is not an attack; instead, Peterson's union may feel encouraged that they are closer than any other union to operating with the following **principles for anti-racist unionism**, which must be included alongside other core issues that impact public education:

- Educators must place eradicating racism in public education at the forefront of the union agenda.

- Educators must work together to eradicate existing barriers that prevent the inclusion of educators of color in the teaching profession.

- Unions must make routine assessments of conditions for students and staff of color part of their bi-annual processes, and take guidance from the voices of communities of color.

- Unions must elect community and parent representatives from communities of color to ensure that student populations of color are included in union decisions.

- Unions must work to extract Eurocentric structural modalities that rely on hierarchy to function, both from union operations and public school systems.

For the most part, union leadership operates in a slightly more democratic manner than district leadership, as union leaders are at least voted into office. Also, many unions utilize a system in which building leaders continue to teach while providing communication and leadership on union issues for fellow teachers who aren't as directly involved. Unions also take feedback from their members through bargaining surveys that, arguably, use a democratic process to identify critical issues that union members wish for the leadership to address (or protect) in the bargaining process.

We must problematize this process by examining the role of whiteness in decision making. If the teaching population is 82% white or higher, we can only expect that the values expressed by teachers in the "democratic" survey process will be, largely if not entirely, be values that protect the greater fabric of white supremacy in the United States. The second principle of anti-racist unionism, fighting barriers facing Black, Latino, and Native American people in the process of becoming teachers, must be addressed before unions can fully move beyond acting as agents of white supremacy. Only when the voices of teachers of color are included at rates that reflect our student populations—which are now quickly moving beyond 50%--will unions function as armies against corporate control and racism in public education.

In writing this, I wonder what fears people have about including more Black, Latino, and Native American teachers in the system. These fears are evident in the refusal of

A DIFFERENT VISION

state teacher testing and certification programs to offer tests in alternative languages (Spanish, for example). Fear is evident in the inability of the public to see that recruiting educators of color will require large-scale initiatives that cost money. Fear is evident in the lack of forward motion and urgency about making schools safe places for students of color—*since these same educators often experienced racism and pain inside of schools, why would they want to return?* I believe that an underlying fear exists about the inclusion of teachers of color in public education. *If we include more teachers of color, will they be able to reach students of color better than white educators—making my teaching style irrelevant? Will they transform the discipline system in a way that will no longer permit, me, the white educator, to utilize humiliation and exclusion to control my students—making the system I use to gain power and control over my classroom irrelevant? Will they teach subject matter that counters what I am teaching, altering the landscape of white supremacy that I benefit from? Will they, due to exclusion from science and mathematics that they experienced, make science and mathematics irrelevant, and place supremacy on teaching ethnic studies? Will they question the way that I relate to (or don't relate to) students of color—ultimately punishing me and humiliating me for the ways I have punished and humiliated students of color for years? Will they transform the system in a way that will make me, the white educator, irrelevant?* As I write these words, I do not mean to contend that these questions even surface in the minds of most white educators. They may be unconscious fears that are operant in the underground, racist, sublevel closet of a collective consciousness that continues to seek, educate, promote, and employ the white educator in the United States.

Some may argue that the movement to include teachers of color in public education is not the job of teachers. Many would assume that this is an administrative responsibility. The failure of teachers to bring this issue to light represents a classic use of silent acceptance to continue a form of racist exclusion that benefits whites. Whites benefit from the exclusion of teachers of color because whites get the jobs, benefits, salaries, and retirement packages instead. Whites continue to empower ourselves economically, maintaining control of public schools, holding the status quo, and silently moving forward in a system that we know is corrupt while taking advantage of its benefits. Our futile protests of our school districts, mostly aimed at maintaining our mediocrity while holding onto our various benefits continue to sooth the parts of us that detect corruption; our collective silence regarding the lack of educators of color helps to promote our supremacy, and thereby the mass exclusion of children of color. If we want to change, we must wake up to reality; our unions are too docile when it comes to fighting for the civil rights of the children we serve; if we genuinely desire to transform the system, we must reinvigorate these sleeping giants to create a mass appeal for racial justice in U.S. schools.

9

The War for Funding

___

How many millions of stories could we tell about the failure of school funding in the United States? For every unserved child, there is a story. There are the stories of children excluded from their education in Flint, Michigan due to lead in their water; there are the stories of teachers photocopying pages from one available AP Biology book to teach 90 eager students in Portland, Oregon; there are stories of one school counselor serving 400 students in hundreds of districts throughout the nation; there are the stories of 40 students in first- grade classrooms with one teacher desperately trying, yet failing, to teach literacy. There are stories of flooded bathrooms; libraries closed due to lack of funding for staff, and instruments locked up in rooms for years due to the cancellation of music programs. These stories are not isolated incidents. They are a well-documented, public, national disgrace. As educators, students, administrators, legislators, and community members, these stories are our stories. If we fail to make changes, to write a new story in which we fund public education in the United States, we must admit our collective authorship of an immense tragedy.

The Funding Labyrinth

Many have written about the factory model of education—popularized in the United States as early as the 1920s and

30s, blooming after World War II, and exploding into present school-to-prison-industrial-complex. The only feature of the aforementioned complex that is not yet fully mature is the complete takeover of public education by corporations—a melt that is happening more slowly, arguably, due to the presence of teachers unions that at very least protect the concept that education must remain free and public. Of course, the term "testocracy" indicates the degree to which aspects of our system, like assessment, have already matured into techno-capitalist tentacles that apply suction to the crumbling public system, simultaneously sucking the funding from our schools, precious time from our teachers, and the brilliant creativity of our children. Still, the system as a whole continues to operate on a highly inequitable system of public funding. Ours is a system so flawed that mushrooms bloom inside classrooms in inner-city Detroit, where the students are 83% Black, while upper-middle-class white students in Gresham, Oregon swipe a card for entrance into their posh gymnasium.

The elaborate maze that is the U.S. system of school funding operates in the following manner: Schools and districts receive state and federal dollars to fund schools—but the majority of funding for public education comes in at the state level. State funding comes from sales and income tax; local funding for schools comes from property tax regulations, which school boards and locally elected politicians prioritize. Inequity in funding, therefore, is inevitable based on the variations of poverty levels in different states; within those states, there is even greater inequity based on district. Students in the Southern States that contend with extreme poverty have less available funding for public education; impoverished districts within those states will experience de facto inequity based on the economic level of the population of that district. For example, students in an impoverished, racially marginalized district in Alabama or Arizona (according to a report by Governing the States and Localities, based on U.S. Census data, these two states spend less per pupil than almost any other state, at, respectively, $8775 and $7,208 per pupil, per year) will automatically experience reduced services. Contrastingly, students in Greenwich, Connecticut (an exceptionally wealthy community in a state that spends $16,631 per pupil) receive greater access to services through public funding and the additional resources that their parents and community donors pump into their schools. This means that correlations between race and poverty within a given state equate to a link between race and poverty in their educational institutions. Those who have the least face additional barriers, like institutional racism within the school system, and the most significant economic barriers at the state, district, and school levels.

In addition to accessing state funds for education, districts can apply for federal grant programs, often based on the level of socio-economic need of their students. This needs-based system is flawed. Instead of automatically providing aid to economically vulnerable schools in a comprehensive way (by looking at property and income tax averages across the United States), the Federal Government establishes grant programs that require incredible resources to apply for and constantly report out on. Large portions of federal grants received by school districts go directly toward administrative costs, administrative salaries for those at the district level who "over-see" grant funds, as well as contracts with organizations who evaluate whether or not funds are properly spent. That grant evaluation and reporting have a well-paid niche in public education, is demonstrative of the level of corruption, mismanagement, and abhorrent priorities that serve upper-middle-class, mostly white middle-managers (who are employed in school systems or federal grant programs) rather than funneling the money more directly to the students in need. Caitlin Emma wrote in her 2015 article, "Here's Why $7 Billion Didn't Help America's Worst Schools,"

> The administration pumped $3 billion of economic stimulus money into the School Improvement Grants program. Six years later, the program has failed to produce the dramatic results the administration had hoped to achieve. About two thirds of SIG schools nationwide made modest or no gains — not much different from similarly bad schools that got no money at all. About a third of the schools actually got worse.

This unfortunate reality is not a castigation against the Obama Administration as much as it is a siren call to revamp the district leadership and grant management models that tend to pay for administrative positions, failing to include teachers, parents, and students in the decision-making process.

My personal experience is another source of information for this issue. I helped to win the 2.5 million dollar SLC-PREP grant for two high schools in Portland Public Schools during the 2006-07 school year. The grant, which ran for five years, did have one excellent feature: it required a teacher signature *and* an administrative signature for all purchases. This meant that a fellow teacher, Pam Garrett, and I worked as half-time grant managers to ensure that as much of the funding as possible went directly to the students. We soon found out that funds from the grant were being used to pay portions of our salaries, as well as a portion of the district grant writer's salary—as she was the individual responsible, ultimately, for reporting back the Federal Government on our progress. As if this wasn't enough, funding was also directed toward middle and lower management. We also contracted with a grant evaluation team, paid for through the grant itself, to oversee our work and report back on our progress. This service was required by the Federal Government to ensure that funds were used responsibly. Fortunately, they were. We used the remaining funds to establish a tutoring center, our Link Crew Program, and the nationally recognized Advanced Scholar Program. However—I bore witness to a level of legal skimming—in the name of integrity and accountability—that evidences the misdirection of funds toward the power structure and away from the students.

The current process that requires impoverished schools and districts to apply for federal funding also comes with well-known strings attached. The requirement is, in most cases, to report out on assessment data—and utilize particular forms of assessment deemed acceptable. Acceptable assessments are dictated by the perceived need for standardization and the existing corporate relationships between big testing, big data, and big ed. money (my name for federal grantmakers). Receiving a Federal Grant, then, means submission to the testocracy, willingness to submit students to months and years of testing that has been proven to be culturally biased to the advantage of white students, and simply put—removal of the student from the opportunity to learn from their teacher to sit in a room and test. Once again, the theme of imprisonment—forced submission to a place by a power greater than one's self—rears its ugly head. Students may "opt-out" of testing; however, this option is not publicized by schools in multiple languages, nor is it in the interest of the school to make this option available. Thus, kids suffer while the biggest profiteers remain federal and middle managers who rake in cozy salaries as overseers of the testocracy, in the process holding the threatening whip of removal of funds and services. This is the cobra clutch of big ed. money—and for kids, there is no escape, other than self-exclusion, or in laymen's terms, just not coming to school.

In this NO EXIT scenario, many schools and districts now look to corporate funding for support. Corporate funding, especially at the local level, can provide much-needed temporary solutions for problems facing schools. For example, around the time our federal SLC-PREP funds ran out, I received a National Education Association Human and Civil Rights Award for opening the doors for African American, Latino, and Native American children in AP courses. When we were struggling the most, I received national recognition for my work. This recognition provided me with the opportunity to express the dire need to continue the work publically. In response, Nike School Innovation Fund came in with $30,000, which allowed us to continue the program for another year. Their support also helped catalyze the demand for Portland Public Schools to find a way to continue the support for our project, which they did by providing an annual budget of $50,000. Nike School Innovation Fund continued to support our work through donations of t-shirts, printing, financial resources, and space to meet. They could not, however, promise stable and complete funding for the entire program. Thus, it is essential that the responsibility for public education does not fall on the shoulders of corporations. A corporation's goal is to amass profit, while they might like to help solve social problems, they cannot be responsible for operating our public schools with a level of integrity that will exceed their self-interest. Ultimately, we must demand a fully funded system in which funds are equitably distributed so that corporate support is never relied on to sustain public programs.

The introduction of for-profit and/or "non-profit" charter schools that operate in conjunction with the public system, use public resources, but often provide lower quality services than traditional public schools is another issue. A recent article, *Race and the Charter School Movement*, published by the New York Collective of Radical Educators (NYCORE), asserts that Black students are choosing charter schools as an alternative to traditional public schools. "Recent studies indicate that a significant number of charter schools perform, similarly, or worse than their matched-public schools…*Blacks make up 30% of the enrollment in the school system, but 60% of the enrollment of charter schools.*" The studies that NYCORE sites established how charter schools promote race-based exclusion in New York State and nationally. This does not necessarily mean that Black children are missing out on a better opportunity. It does mean that public funds are being used to promote exclusion and race-based segregation, thereby draining limited available funds for public schools where Black children attend, in order to promote exclusionary opportunities that benefit, primarily, white children.

Questions for Reflection:

1. What does your state spend, per pupil annually?
2. How does this amount compare with education spending in other states?
3. How does school funding differ from town to town and neighborhood to neighborhood in your state? Spend some time researching and writing about the disparities in your area.
4. How are African American, Latino, and Native American children in your state impacted by geographic and economic marginalization in education?
5. How do white children in middle class and upper-middle-class communities benefit from greater access to resources in your state? Which communities or neighborhoods profit the most from the system of race & geography-based marginalization?
6. Which legislators can you contact to make a statement about these disparities?
7. Would you consider writing a letter to the parent-teacher organizations in the wealthiest communities, to highlight the disparities that result in greater privileges for their children and create pressure for social change?

Hope for a Revitalized, Equitable Funding Structure

The system of funding for public education is a frightening enigma. It is eagerly waiting at the gates to rob the nation's children of resources before they can access them. What is the antidote to its painful and exacting sting? Naming, understanding, and communicating about systemic barriers is an essential aspect of finding the balm (or whole medicine cabinet of salves, balms, and other natural remedies) that will heal them. As activists, community members, parents, and educators, we must understand and name the problem, and remain hopeful that we can find our way out of the labyrinthine puzzle where we find ourselves. If we cannot move forward with that hope, we cannot place our children and future generations inside the belly of the beast and walk away with an unburdened conscience.

What solutions exist to provide consistent funding for public education so we can create schools that all children can attend, with the expectation of equitable opportunities and outcomes? We cannot sincerely answer this question without first eradicating racism from our society. Regardless of the civil rights legislation of past years that mandates the end of segregation and inequality, we continue to see white parents make an effort to exclude their children from the experience of attending school with Black, Latino, and Native American children. This is seen in the charter school movement, but it also plays out in every public school district throughout the country. The current psycho-conservative white power movement that became more visible during the 2016 Republican primaries is a perfect example of the latent racism that is behind to varying degrees, the desire of many white families to remain segregated from Black, Latino, and Native American people. Charlottesville reminds us that the battles won during the civil rights era were legal battles—not cultural or moral battles. These were battles that many whites felt they had *lost* while leaders of color celebrated a few hard-won wins. Civil rights victories do not mean cultural or ideological victories; in fact, it seems that they fueled the flames of resentment for many whites. While this may feel hopeless to readers, it is necessary to accept and understand the actual status of racist consciousness in the United States—and then work forward from there. Buried resentments do not lead to social change. They lead to explosion, or to covert action that maintains white power—like furtively figuring out loopholes in the system that ensure one's white children will not cross the bridge to attend school with Black and Latino youth; or, like funding and supporting school board candidates who will retain the structure of white supremacy by overlooking civil rights legislation in order to prioritize the legacy of white power in historically white, privileged schools.

Furthermore, do Black, Latino, and Native American parents facing this segregation, either within schools due to upper tier courses being reserved for white students or within districts—where one school is historically located as the brown school and the other the white school, actually wish for their children to attend these schools that are bastions of white privilege? Perhaps not! We cannot fix or revolutionize our public education system unless we extract racism from the landscape of U.S. identity and consciousness. Thus, we can only dream of how schools could be—and doing so must involve an entire reimagination of the meaning of school, and that dream must come from the empowered voices of our communities of color.

While moving beyond racism must occur to rectify barriers to equitable funding, we must also take practical steps in our local communities, and at the state and federal levels, to ensure that current funds and properly utilized for the benefit of young people. Here are a series of actions that individuals in society can take to improve the flow of funding to education, right away.

Public Accountability Initiatives for Federal Grants

Members of the public have the right to view a great deal more information than they ever see. For example, most federal grants require significant, annual grant reporting. District staff complete the federal grant reports and then send them to the Federal Government for review. Members of the public may request information from their school board or the office of the superintendent on all federal grants. We can read the "grant narratives," which describe the intended purpose of a federal grant. We can also request the opportunity to read and review the annual federal grant report. Often, even when districts have not properly utilized funds, they may submit a plan-of-action that indicates how they will rectify errors and move forward in a manner that is in line with the goals of the federal grant. These plans to rectify errors or misspending may disguise inappropriate uses of funds, allowing district administrators to use creative language so that their district continues to receive federal dollars. There is no reason why members of the public cannot see the federal grant report, and the Federal Government's response. These are public documents that must be made available upon request. While Districts may not be prepared for mass requests for grant reporting documents, even the efficacy shown by *making such a request* will help to improve the accountability around spending. If you ask your district for such information, and they refuse to show you the information, what reason do they give for preventing members of the public from viewing it? If members of the public request public documents and are denied, they can also contact the media for help, stating that a request for public information was denied. When district officials are forthcoming with grant documents, members of the public may soon notice the funds that are spent on administrative salaries, travel, and other items that have no relationship to the grant goals. It is important that the public ask questions regarding these expenditures, as asking for answers from our leaders is an action we can take to begin the process of restoring trust and accountability in our system. Members of the public may also contact the federal offices that receive and review these grant reports to either make a complaint or declare a need for priorities to be refocused toward the community and the children. Often, grant language seems so complicated that members of the public may feel alienated in reading it. However, writing back from a place of alienation to ask questions regarding how and where funds are being used to support young people is a totally appropriate course of action that will help to hedge spending on the side of our children, rather than allowing egregious budgeting that benefits top-heavy administrations to fly under the radar.

Public Accountability for State Spending on Education

We can also easily look up our state legislators, including our congressional leaders, our senators, governors, and our state superintendent of education and their staff. We can craft an email that requests information on where to locate the state budget for public education. In this process, we may encounter administrative assistants who can direct us to the right webpage, or we may encounter the spin cycle of legislative chaos that fails to provide the kind of document the public can interpret. The crevasse between those who can interpret budget language and those who cannot is wide and deep; instead of giving up, it is paramount that we, as educators, activists, and parents, request that documentation regarding education spending is available immediately, and in multiple languages. Once again, while attempts to gather information may not be instantly fruitful, the process of requesting it, especially if multiple parents and community members write requests, can add accountability to both funding choices and how our institutions communicate funding choices to the public. Parents and community members who wish to make a more substantial dent in how their state funds education may wish to unite to request the regular publication of budget reports that succinctly details expenditures.

District Budget Process Review – Use Social Media to Improve Accountability

Many school districts hold annual budget review sessions where members of the public may attend to lobby for the continuation of spending in a particular area, or for the addition of funding for an innovative project. In most locales, the school board ultimately approves or disapproves the budget. This process tends to marginalize members of the community who cannot spend additional time showing up to the school board meeting due to employment and community members who do not speak English. Nationally, we have tremendous work to do in ensuring equity of access both to the process and to the budget documents themselves. One way that we can move forward to make the process more transparent is by requiring school districts to publish a clear synopsis of the line-item budget in multiple languages on the district website in a manner that can be shared via social media. Doing so will allow heightened accountability by widening the audience and thereby opening the doors for traditionally marginalized communities to speak up regarding unmet needs. Perhaps the first step, then, is to request revision of the process by which budget information is made public. In the age of social media, a document is not public because it is available at a school board meeting. Making something public must mean that it can be easily circulated in the community. Twitter hashtags and other forms of tech-activism can be used to lobby for specific budget alterations, needs, and shifts in priorities. School board members are elected officials who communities must hold accountable not only while they are seated at their podiums, but also through the variety of resources available through social media.

Imprisoned Funds

Greater accountability for existing federal, state, and local education budgets, arguably, only shines a light on one aspect of the corruption. The discussion of public education funding cannot be divorced from the conversation about dramatic increases in funding for for-profit prisons that hold both youth and adults in all parts of the United States. In Rebecca Klein's article, "States are Prioritizing Prisons Over Education, Budgets Show," she writes,

> A report released by the Center on Budget and Policy Priorities shows that the growth of state spending on prisons in recent years has outpaced the growth of spending on education. After adjusting for inflation, state general-fund spending on prison-related expenses increased over 140 percent between 1986 and 2013. During that same period, state K-12 spending on education increased only 69%...

In juxtaposing our well-funded system of mass incarceration with our poorly funded public schools, I realize that the dynamics I present paint a pitiful and depressing picture. One editor asked me to consider utilizing a more hopeful tone, to perhaps color in the spaces between words with more positive notes, painting a picture of what we can be, rather than dwelling in the negative reality of what we, as a system, are today. When I think of my former students who are currently locked away, both African American males, I cannot don a happy face. When I read the staggering data presented in Michelle Alexander's *The New Jim Crow*, which shows how mass incarceration disproportionately impacts men of color, I cannot alter my tone to take the reader to a happy place. Instead, my hope comes from a much deeper belief that by acknowledging these haunting, latent truths about our society, we are taking the first steps toward change.

The United States currently incarcerates more people than any other nation in the world; I cannot offer the reader rose-colored glasses. I invite you to walk with me through the treacherous reality enveloping us—we pay for the most extensive system of incarceration, imprisoning more young people than any other nation. For me, the truth is deeply hopeful. Envisioning, remembering, and writing about the millions of people currently locked in cells in sub-sub-urban and rural areas of our nation gives me hope that by seeing and acknowledging this awful reality, we can work together to unlock the cells and let them out. I am, of course, not so naïve to think that this will happen with any immediacy, but I cannot exist in a reality where I pretend that mass incarceration is not happening, and exclude this essential reality from a book about the transformation of public education. A question that I first learned about in the fifth grade, while studying the Holocaust—if German citizens knew about concentration camps, even if they knew about them as "work camps," why didn't more reject the systemic marginalization and murder that happened inside? When I think about the 2.3 million incarcerated people in state, federal, and juvenile facilities and local jails, according to the Prison Policy Initiative, I cannot help but wonder how we, as fellow human beings, are allowing this huge number of people to go on living locked away in the shadows of our society. When I add to the picture that private prisons and youth facilities profit greatly through operating prisons that hold the greatest number of jailed people in human history, I have trouble sleeping at night. When I consider that 34,000 of these individuals are in youth facilities (and another 20,000 are excluded from the data because they are held in residential facilities), also disproportionality Black and Brown, I cannot stand the thought of moving forward with life without living in protest of this system. When I accept that the majority of incarcerated youth are locked up for non-violent offenses, and 7000 are locked up for "technical violations" (like parole violations), it becomes clear that the restructuring of the criminal justice system, by closing prisons and ending the for-profit prison system, must be part of the vision for a transformed system of public education. For as long as we, as a society, allow our prison system to exist as a gargantuan vortex that sucks the life and resources out of our society, we cannot expect the funds we need to appear for public schools. Likewise, until the prison system is shut down, it will continue to reach its tentacles into our schools, seeking the most vulnerable young people to incarcerate, institutionalize, and feed on.

The problem, at times, seems so magnificent that any solution appears implausible. How could we possibly fight such a monolithic culture of incarceration? How could we change a system run by such powerful, wealthy individuals who have major contracts in every state? How can we challenge the concept that imprisonment aids society by protecting citizens from evil-doers? How can we shut down the brand new prison that we just paid millions to build in towns X, Y, and Z? While these and many other obstacles can make change seem impossible, I harken back to the destruction of the institution of slavery in the Southern States in the United States. I remember the Berlin Wall falling. I think about the invasion of the concentration camps in Germany and Poland. I have to believe that, though very difficult, magnificent change is possible. I have to believe that, with the right leadership and with the right organization of human intention, change is inevitable. The changes that we need to make to restructure this system totally will seem outlandish when first presented. They will seem implausible, as we cannot currently see how we get from our current nadir to the seemingly utopian zenith that remains illusory, ethereal, and hard to grasp. But in the interest of believing in *a* future, I must continue to describe this hopeful vision.

The arduous work required to build a society that prevents mass incarceration by providing gainful and meaningful employment, and by providing a functional system of public education that prepares people for that bright future will require a significant shift in our means of production and our system of employment. As a whole, we must reinvest in the society through a massive movement toward employment of our people in public works projects. Including total redesign of our high schools (which will be discussed in a later chapter), nationally, a societal move toward sustainability in all homes and buildings through geothermal heat, and solar energy, and conservative and aggressive recycling and composting programs, a system of high speed trains, and a system-wide movement toward sustainable urban and suburban agriculture. Reinvestment in sustainable public infrastructure will create meaningful labor for many years—and new jobs will continue to be available through the investment that our society needs to make in itself. Only a large-scale federal investment in sustainability can produce the kind of labor demand needed to offset the dysfunctional labor vacuum of the current prison system itself. Where will the money come from? Well, why can't funds come from a Federal commitment to reinvest dollars invested in for-profit prisons into the creation of a modernized, sustainable national infrastructure?

Many members of the American public seem to feel so entrenched in the system that surrounds them that they cannot imagine how to dig themselves out. But we have to do just that—dig ourselves out of this negative cycle through re-establishing the way that our country interacts with the earth. All of the technology needed to create a more sustainable society is readily available; it is time to turn the lights on and eradicate the deadly systems of oppression that will otherwise continue a cycle of imprisonment and Apartheid. According to the PEW Charitable Trust, 80% of Americans are currently in debt. This debt originates from mortgages, credit cards, and student loan debt—all of which force the society as a whole into a noxious state of consciousness where self-interest and anxiety prevail. It is no wonder that there is a mass addiction to prescription anxiety drugs (like Xanax)—even those who do not live behind prison walls are imprisoned in the cycle of debt that keeps many in misery, and prevents the society as a whole from viewing the cycle for what it is—dysfunctional, cruel, racist, harmful to the planet and its inhabitants.

It is more than time for a new paradigm—it is a time for an entirely new state of consciousness. Like any other moment in human history when sizable change is required, part of this shift will come from willing participants who come together to lead in a new direction. The other part of the shift will result from conflict between profiteers who wish to maintain their vice grip and those who suffer the most. This dramatic conflict is being staged before our eyes through the murder of innocent (often Black or Latino) people by police, through the threatening lunacy of Donald Trump and his white power revolution.

As educators, parents, community leaders, and activists, we must move forward proactively both through protest and by creating landing pads where a new anti-racist, sustainable, humanitarian consciousness can thrive. This merely means moving forward with faith to organize our communities into safe zones, involving sustainable practices in our activist projects, building and maintaining sustainable relationships centered on core principles that celebrate and empower humanity at the nexus of racial and environmental justice. These key principles could be:

Key Principles at the Nexus of Environmental and Racial Justice

1. We acknowledge the violent, brutal history of white supremacy and white European domination. We do not tolerate white supremacy or any form of race-based social organization that privileges one "race" over another.

2. We acknowledge the continued destructive impact of colonialism on planet earth. We seek every opportunity to live in harmony with the planet, viewing pollution of the Earth as part of the colonial domination of consciousness.

3. We reject the school-to-prison pipeline. We view mass incarceration as a crime against humanity. We demand that the U.S. government stop investing in this prison system. We seek help from the United Nations to declare that the investment of public funds in for-profit prisons is a crime against humanity.

4. We seek the opportunity to begin again with a redesigned concept of public education that utilizes the best anti-racist pedagogical philosophy and the most effective (non-corporate) educational technology, always premised in sustainable practices, to create a system of education that promotes personal liberation, empowerment, and true innovation.

5. We demand that the U.S. government reinvest money spent on mass incarceration into the complete redesign of public education. We demand that Black, Latino, and Native American education and sustainability leaders and activists play key roles in the envisioning process. We demand inclusion of teachers and administrative staff of color at rates comparable to the communities being served.

Public education funding is a multi-layered puzzle, but we can only find our way out by examining and accepting the embedded dynamics that make the system dysfunctional. When we gather together to discuss these dynamics—whether it is two families talking in the backyard about how debt impacts their choices or a community meeting about the impact of mass incarceration, we begin to move consciousness. Respectability politics—in this case, the concept that we should be ashamed if we are in debt, if we have family members who are incarcerated, if our child is facing problems in a racist school system, trap us in a state of secrecy and humiliation that inhibits our communication, and keeps us locked into a system that perpetuates white supremacy, white economic domination, and the total control of our economic status, and of the way we feel about ourselves and one another. We can start to walk away from these feelings by openly discussing how different aspects of the system affect us. These discussions can lead to community alliances, built on the power of human individuals who are moving together in trust and out of love, which will have the power to move society forward. So through it all, keep communing. Keep listening to your neighbor. Keep building fires in your backyards, loving one another, keep protesting, and keep believing in the possibility of a better world.

Questions for Reflection & Discussion:

Following are some questions for discussion. These might be useful for a discussion between educators in a school setting, or between neighbors at a get-together or community meeting.

1. How does debt impact our community? How are individuals of this community impacted by debt?

What feelings arise regarding debt?

2. How does mass incarceration impact our community? How are individual members harmed by the system of mass incarceration? What feelings come up when we discuss mass incarceration?

3. How is our community impacted by funding (or lack thereof) for public education? How are children harmed by the failure to fund public education?

4. What kinds of questions could we ask our state and local legislators regarding the budget? What specific funds would we like to see reprioritized? Who among us is willing to take part in an email/ social media campaign to demand accountability in public funding? Who will start the Facebook group? Who is willing to help to circulate our message? Who is willing to host meetings? Who is willing to attend school board meetings? Who wishes to participate and like and share our posts? What other groups could we align with, support, or receive support from?

Like sparrows, we must gather together in our smallness until our presence creates an undeniable demand for full civil rights now. We must demand an end to all practices that are unsustainable, unjust, racist, anti-Earth, and inhumane. We must demand that every piece of legislation that is currently being ignored or overlooked is enacted and respected as law. However, when we sail forward through the rough waters of this journey, we are bound to see waves of racism that attempt to pull us back to our Jim Crow institutions. When we encounter these waves, we must stay together, utilizing our voices, cameras, and social media to document every civil rights violation. Our documentation will serve as evidence for the need of a new, alternative system that we create—resting in the truth that our Euro-centric system is rooted in colonialism and brutality against the earth and its inhabitants and therefore will not serve us. We must destroy to rebuild.

10

School Design for a New Humanity

When I creaked open the door of my new classroom in 2003, I was surprised to see rat feces and chipping paint littering the floor. Desperate to begin my first teaching job and a bit afraid to begin by complaining to the administration, I found a broom and swept the room—my entree into a cycle that requires teachers to sweep away and hide harmful features of the system. That position, at Franklin High School, provided an incredible lesson in the limits of teacher power.

Between 2003 and 2016, my solitary focus was revitalizing the school by creating a culture of academic success. I worked with more than ten different administrators throughout those 12 years, yet my fellow teachers, counselors, and I continued to operate several transformative programs. Including the program, I spearheaded and energized—the Advanced Scholar Program (described in detail in the Appendix). I reached a level of community-based support that was threatening to the hierarchical structure. When I challenged proposals that would return us to antiquated systems that would harm students and end our progress, I found myself battling with the administration. They made numerous moves to cut down my capacity, including placing my office in-between two rooms with no access to the outside building—literally trapping me, so students had trouble accessing me.

After years of success (including local, state, and national awards), I decided to depart before administrative choices destroyed the good work before my eyes. Leaving was not an easy choice—I spent thirteen years of my life working beyond myself to revolutionize the school. Surrendering to the reality that a new administration could come in and destroy my work and the work of my colleagues, despite significant support from communities of color, was absolutely heartbreaking. I departed with the realization that I never failed as a leader, but most administrators felt entitled to garner all of the power for themselves, leaving no room for authentic teacher leadership.

One month after I decided to transfer to another school and start over in my beloved role of classroom teacher, the local media broke the story—Portland Public Schools water was full of lead. Over 80 schools tested positive for lead in the water, and high-level administrators knew about it but chose not inform the public. Throughout my crusade to create a functional school system that would empower young people of color, I was drinking lead alongside my students. Throughout my period of, admittedly, work addiction in the name of social justice, I also drank lead-infested water while pregnant. Soon, the media revealed that a faucet in my new school contained water with four times the amount of lead found in faucets in Flint, Michigan. They also discovered neuro-toxic lead paint chips and dust in dozens of schools.

This hard-earned life lesson was one of multi-faceted irony—regardless of how revolutionary I thought I was, the system's failure impacted me as a worker, a human being, and a mother. I could not cure the school system of educational inequity through excellent programming. No amount of love, passion, or empowerment can contend with poison in the water, and poison floating in the air. Moreover, that this can occur in Portland, Oregon—one of the wealthiest cities in the United States—is a case study of the national public health crisis we face due to the failure to invest in public infrastructure. It's time to rebuild the system from the ground up, this time with a focus on sustainability and racial justice, making amends to the planet, and to the communities most frequently harmed. To rebuild with the right priorities, we must analyze the history of school design in the United States.

Institutions built for Social Control

How does the current architecture of U.S. schools reflect hierarchy, white supremacy, and factory education? What will school buildings look like in a re-envisioned system? The 2012 work, *A History of School Design and Its Indoor Environmental Standards, 1900 to Today*, by then PhD Candidate in the Department of Architecture's Center for the Built Environment at UC Berkeley, Lindsay Baker, offers a thorough and direct examination of the history of school design in the United States, as well as a brief inquiry into the future of school architecture. To focus this chapter on how school architecture can be a tool for racial justice, we must, firstly, understand how current school and classroom structures offer ideal locations for teaching racial injustice.

Near the beginning of her work, Baker notes:

An early model for the standard adequate classroom was drawn up by Horace Mann, an early
educational reformer, which called for standard
rows of desks, windows on two sides of the room,
and a variety of other necessary amenities. It was
this movement, known as the Common School
movement, which popularized the notion of free
schools paid for by local property taxes, which
grew over time in the first half of the 19th century
across the country.

Mann's intention—primarily to implement his free
schools and pay for them through property taxes—remains
the cornerstone of U.S. of public education. Likewise, his
vision of the classroom—rows of desks, windows, and
a teacher at the front of the room remains the primary
instructional model. We must credit Mann for setting the
concept of free and public education into stone; we must
also remember that the schools he set out to establish *were
never meant to serve non-white students.* Mann's schools
were distinctly designed to benefit property owning whites.
He saw a social need, had a vision for implementation,
found public support from property-owning whites, and
began designing a model for education that we continue
to operate inside of.

Mann's model perfectly embodies what Paulo Freire
called the banking concept of education. In Chapter 2, page
1 of his highly-acclaimed book, *Pedagogy of the Oppressed*,
Freire writes:

> Education thus becomes an act of depositing, in
> which the students are the depositories and the
> teacher is the depositor. Instead of communicat-
> ing, the teacher issues communiques and makes
> deposits which the students patiently receive,
> memorize, and repeat. This is the "banking' con-
> cept of education, in which the scope of action
> allowed to the students extends only as far as
> receiving, filing, and storing the deposits.

The problem with this structure, Freire theorizes, is its promotion of students as lesser than the educator, thereby promoting oppression. Racism further exacerbates this dynamic. While the power differential would still exist in a similar set-up room with a white teacher and white students, the pre-existing structure of white supremacy and structural racism magnifies this dynamic. Our 82% white teaching force, principally functions within Mann's model which was designed in the early 19th century to support the children of landowning whites. Before lessons even begin, classrooms perpetuate classism and racism due to set-up. If we give our well-intentioned educators the benefit of the doubt, we accept that they do not have power over the design of their classroom, the schedule that students follow, the level of physical activity that students get, or the furniture in the room. Changing this factor, then, will require social pressure to examine the role of race in school design and to provide spaces that consider the needs of diverse communities, as well as how new schools can attract more educators of color, and be comfortable community centers for Black, Latino, and Native American parents and families.

In her examination of the history of school design, Baker describes shifts throughout the post-war era and then continued shifts throughout the 1970s. While many alternative ideas about school design continue to be considered, there is little written about the role of linguistic and racial diversity in school architecture and classroom design. While current designers continue to examine how schools could be more sustainable, the discussion on school design for the future centers around how to involve new technology, how to conserve resources, and how to create a positive learning environment for a generic, homogenous set of students. The discussion rarely, if ever, moves toward analysis of race. For example, how the arrangement of desks, homogenous patterning, and power dynamic create uncomfortable feelings of confinement for all students, especially Black, Latino, and Native American students whose feelings of confinement are compounded by the *reality of confinement* inside a structurally and culturally racist system?

The current focuses of school redesign are not necessarily harmful to Black, Latino, and Native American students—except that these students are the least likely to experience the cutting edge, brand-new school buildings of the future. However, it is imperative to consider what factors must be deliberated to create schools that serve and protect both the natural environment and the people that will populate these new buildings. If we are to reach toward the nexus between environmental justice and racial justice as we rebuild our schools, we must develop a nuanced understanding of what racial justice in school design even looks like. Following is a list of principles for anti-racist school design. These principles are meant to be critiqued, discussed, added to, and used to further the conversation.

Principles for Anti-Racist School Design at the Building Level

- School structures must include meeting places where specific cultural communities can meet to discuss and plan events, uninterrupted, in their own language.

- Schools must contain an auditory information system that provides an automatic translation (or where students or parents may press a button for a translated version) like in airports.

- School structures must contain an area where adults may convene with students to plant community gardens, harvest, and cook food that celebrates student culture.

- Schools must contain signage in the major language groups of the school population.

- School buildings must contain visual displays that can be changed each year to reflect images of current, successful students, as well as images of historical figures that represent successful aspects of various cultural communities.

- Community garden crops must reflect the diets and recipes of the multiple school community members. Information regarding community use of the garden must be posted in multiple languages.

- Movement practices of multiple communities must be reflected in the physical fitness design. Physical fitness design must not be segregated into one building; instead, a focus on fitness and movement must exist throughout the entire school. Designers must survey the entire community regarding preferred movement activities. If so, are there spaces available on every floor and in every hall for movement breaks—nerf basketball hoops, badminton nets, yoga, Qi Gong, and breakdance floors, for example? Could there be a movement library where students may check out both space and equipment to remain active in all parts of the school?

- How are sound and music incorporated to reflect various cultures? Technology can easily allow for sound-proof spaces where multiple student populations could listen to different music at the same time. Could the concept of "library" be expanded to allow for check out of sound rooms and music as literature?

Other Considerations:

- Could public libraries convene with school libraries to strengthen the public library system, making more books and resources available, and provide community meeting spaces where any parent or authorized family member could access this part of the building while students also occupy it?

- Are there multiple spaces for dance, music, and the celebration of culture? Combined listening and movement rooms could provide for a greater sense of inclusiveness, allowing multiple communities to feel simultaneously included.

Classroom Level

- Classrooms can be redesigned to eradicate teacher-centered instruction and empower students. For example, the creation of multiple speaking platforms in the room, with several designated as sacrosanct for student presentation of material—could shift the dynamic toward a more equitable balance of *who has the floor.*

- Desks and chairs must be easily movable so they may be arranged to benefit community-oriented learning, rather than teacher-centered learning. Furniture must *allow* the teacher to turn the learning away from him or herself.

- The room must encourage comfort. Designers must survey the population to understand indicators of comfort for the cultural communities in the student population.

- Popular sayings, positive maxims, and encouraging phrases and images can be permanent features of the classroom. Designers can survey the school population to gather sayings and images that best reflect the cultural community.

Questions for Reflection:

1. Where do students of color regularly convene in my current school building (or in my children's school)?

2. Do students feel comfortable communicating in their home language in the school environment where I work or where my children attend school?

3. With public schools quickly growing to more than 50% non-white, what factors must designers consider in order to create positive, successful learning environments?

4. How can new technology be applied in a manner that will assist diverse learners and their families in reaching their highest potential as learners and community members?

5. When thinking about the school you work in or send your children to, what would you add to the list of considerations? What would you like to see changed?

6. What specific features or symbols would make you or your child feel comfortable in school?

7. What is the most important design change that can be made to improve the quality of education, in your opinion?

The dysfunctionality of our current system, a level of dysfunction that negatively impacts the minds we wish to empower through public education, provides us with an essential opportunity to move forward. From Portland to Flint, total reconstruction (salvaging historic features where we can) will be required to eliminate asbestos, lead paint, and lead solder inside our schools. The kind of investment required to create buildings that are suitable for human occupancy will require a major commitment from the society as a whole. Rebuilding our schools must be a national priority that is heavily supported by billions in public funding. As usual, the chaotic reality that many of our school buildings are uninhabitable creates a great opportunity to redesign our entire system in a way that actually serves the diverse communities of young people who will occupy them in the future.

The revolution for a new system of public education must prioritize both racial and environmental justice. School buildings can be didactic models of sustainability, with solar power, gardens that provide healthy food for school communities, outdoor classrooms that enrich and empower young people through active biology instruction through seed cultivation, compost and soil quality studies, and micro-nutrient research that can and will reveal food as a healing medicine for our ill society. With school buildings that include features that support cultural communities, and include cultural communities as *leaders* in the design process, students will emerge equipped to lead. We must intend to create a new generation of leaders who think creatively about how to utilize new technology as a healing resource for the injured earth as we make the slow but necessary move from Homo Sapien to Techno-Eco-Sapien—a new species that overcame the greed, domination, cruelty, and supremacy of their predecessors, bringing the world to a new state of harmony and unity by using technology to heal the ecology and love, value, and respect one another's differences. If this ending sounds like science fiction, consider the dystopian reality that is the state of our oceans, our prisons, and our forests. We must break through the brutality of racial hatred, the pressure of patriarchy, and the grasp of capitalist greed to claim a new humanity that fosters an entirely new concept of education.

CONCLUSION

Standing Together in Action

We stand together, teachers, administrators, counselors, policymakers, and community organizers, at a crucial moment in history—a moment when urban areas and small towns are exploding in protest. In this moment where young people of color are being suspended, expelled, and jailed at higher rates than ever it is crucial that we come together to solve the public education crisis. We must harvest the energy of this moment. With great immediacy, let us meditate on the revolutionary intentions of civil rights leaders of decades past, their power and commitment evidenced by their willingness to die, but their *actual deaths* in the name of civil rights. Let's never forget. Let's reread the vision of Frederick Douglass, Dr. King, Reverend Shuttlesworth, Cesar Chavez, Dorothy Cotton, Ida B. Wells, and others. Let's review the core values of our movement while allowing ourselves to be led forward by new leaders who will help us reshape and redefine our new civil rights movement.

Let's move forward together as an army for increased funding and diversity in teaching staffs and leadership, for the inclusion of the voices of all communities in the redesign of our entire system. As teachers, let's move forward by re-examining every single way that our institutions and classrooms promote racism and white supremacy, and the intersecting factors of gender and sexual identity oppression. We have always put in extra energy and worked for moderate to low pay. If we are going to continue doing that anyway, let's step up to the plate of the legacy of civil rights and be a million thorns in the side of those who would prefer to deconstruct and privatize public education entirely. Together, we can produce change that the next generation will recall with great respect.

As teachers who are members of unions, we can no longer operate in a manner that prioritizes our own needs above racial justice. We must include racial justice in our guiding principles, using our solidarity to fight for both our professional needs *and* the needs of the communities we serve.

As empowered, activist administrators, we must make solid connections with fellow administrators who are oriented toward social and racial justice, and commit to doing our jobs as social justice activists. We must align with community members willing to support us, moving beyond the old paradigm that requires us to take directives from above while neglecting the real needs of our school communities. We must be willing to take risks in efforts to create equitable schools.

As parents, we must find ways to meet—either through social media or in our backyards or front stoops, to demand accountability about both racial equity and funding in our children's schools and in our school districts. We must reach beyond the boundaries of race, class, and gender to genuinely embrace members of cultural communities that are different than ours. For whites, this will mean relinquishing many privileges that both empower us economically and politically and segregate us from Black and Brown parents who live and work near us, but are often screened out of the opportunity to participate in the most basic political processed (like attending a PTA meeting) due to economic and social constraints. Instead of demanding that members of these communities meet us in our chosen location at our chosen time, we must strive to include various perspectives in ways that benefit them. This will require communication, sometimes in another language, but we must traverse this crevasse because if we can't then neither can our teachers and neither will our children. If we want a better society, we must reach out, open up, and refuse to operate from our dominance and privilege until our Black and Brown sisters and brothers are seated at the same table, with the same powers and the same privileges to design, to speak and be heard, to vote, and to change our society. Perhaps, we will decide to redesign our political process as well, as it too is rooted in white supremacist patriarchy, but for now—refusing to act without representation from all cultural communities within our schools is a reasonable place to start. We must demand school buildings that, instead of poisoning our children, will support our cultural communities while also operating sustainably. We must see that the only way forward is through the great fire; either we walk together, or we allow it to consume us. For our children, we must continue the forward march of social, racial, and environmental justice.

As activists, we must create places in the community for others to express themselves, enjoy one another's humanity, and learn about tools for social and racial justice organization. We must also refuse to judge those who are not yet involved in our movements, instead continuing to welcome newcomers and share knowledge. If this is difficult, we must remember that many Americans are one paycheck away from realizing how capitalist pressure affects them (often the lights go on when the lights go off). As activists, we must relentlessly measure our survival against the need to place pressure on the system, through protesting the police, protesting exclusion in our political processes, and through convening with other activists to rotate our resistant voices against the power structures we wish to dismantle. Instead of keeping this conversation about self-sacrifice internal, we must externalize it, sharing the dialogue with others who experience the same inner dilemma. Through this meta-conversation, we better know who is best to take which risk, and who may need a short break to stay vital and committed. As elders in the activist movement, we must both share what we know about keeping ourselves safe and leading successful movements and collaborate with youth activists to learn the endless ways we can use the internet and social media as activist tools. We must keep ourselves healthy, resisting depression and isolation through uniting with other activists, remembering to laugh once in a while as we beat our hands against the beast.

We must begin immediately, with great urgency, to address the failure of our educational system. We must organize ourselves and move forward in every town and city, in every school district, with absolute focus and one clear goal: implementing a system with a different vision—one in which all children are curious, beautiful creatures deserving of respect, opportunity, and love. One in which empowerment replaces humiliation, relationships replace control. One in which respect for humanity and our earth are central tenets of both curriculum and the design of our school buildings. Every single one of us is profoundly needed. Let's stand together, cognizant of the past, willing to change, and ready to act on behalf of a new humanity and a new, equitable and sustainable system.

APPENDIX

Advanced Scholars Program, a Case Study of Sorts

As large of a problem as racism is in our country's school system, we can take action against it. I have seen teachers take action—I have been among them—and I have seen the outcomes of such actions. It fills my heart to know that racism in several Portland schools is less prolific than it was a decade ago, to know my fellow educators are making a concerted effort to incorporate equity into their classrooms. But it's not enough. Racism is still pervasive, in my school district and districts nationwide.

This book has provided you with tips for ensuring equity in your classroom and for building relationships with your peers to shift your school culture subtly. I hope your changes can be more than subtle, though. I've been fortunate enough to develop an inclusive AP program at Franklin High School, collaborating with a talented team of teachers and mentors to produce record numbers of students of color excelling in high school, college, and beyond. In this Appendix, I offer the Advanced Scholars Program story as an example, a case study of sorts, of what systemic change can look like. I hope it helps you make lasting change in your school too.

Not Plug 'n' Play

Higher dropout rates, lower test scores, and lower rates of participation in advanced courses are documented realities for Black, Latino, Native American, and Pacific Islander students. Thousands of researchers are currently writing dissertations on the multiple layers of the problem; corporations are peddling strategies to school districts, claiming they will solve these issues as we speak.

I receive countless emails related to workshops I can attend to improve my relationships with students from "diverse" backgrounds. A highly lucrative corporate subculture now shrouds the national educational inequity crisis in a smothering blanket of dysfunction; we know our schools are sick when private corporations and consultants make millions from the desperation inflicted by inequity.

Racism lives in American consciousness, and institutional racism resides in school culture, starting from kindergarten. A national shift in consciousness is required to ameliorate the problem. So as I write, I ask you to separate me from the profiteers accepting public funding to solve problems related to educational equity. There is no plug 'n' play solution for all schools, classrooms, and students, so I approach from a different angle.

I am here to share changes made by teachers at one school, as I have shared teaching strategies that succeeded inside my classroom. I do so with the hope that some of what we have done as an educational community might work for you. But never to suggest that I understand the nuances of your context or that there is one overarching solution for all of us, other than a massive change in the psychology of the nation as a whole...and even then, we would have to eradicate institutional racism, brick by brick.

Overview

At Franklin High School, in Portland, teachers mobilized to eradicate vestiges of institutional racism. In 2007, a small group of teachers noticed that our school had declining enrollment and a low graduation rate, while another neighborhood school had increasing enrollment and a higher graduation rate. Our neighborhood youth were fleeing to that school. When we took a look at the school, it was easy to see that their IB program was taking off, while our AP program had dwindling numbers, and was mostly populated by middle-class white students.

We started our Advanced Scholar's Program (ASP) in the dreamy days of 2007. It grew from 88 students to 465 students taking four or more AP courses. In 2011 a local school was collapsed into ours, increasing our school population more than double and the free and reduced lunch population increased in one fell swoop. Statistically, the increase in the free and reduced lunch population meant a decreased graduation rate, but the graduation rate *increased*. Students came knocking on the door to gain admittance to Franklin High School. Before we started, the reverse was true.

The Oregon Department of Education, the National Education Association, the College Board, and our district recognized our work. We made progress in a particular area—dramatically increasing the number of students of color engaged in, and successful in, AP courses. As a result of this shift, we also had the highest rate of graduation for African American students in the state of Oregon for two years in a row, as well as an increasing graduation rate for Latino students.

We attribute our accomplishments to several reasons. First, we had an excellent administrator, Dr. Charles Hopson (May he rest in peace), whose sole objective was to move the school forward in terms of equity. We had a strong sense of collaboration between the administrator and the teachers (much of which was due to his willingness to encourage our leadership and free thought, while expecting us to bring our ideas back to the table for his approval and to keep the focus on equity) and we had won a $2.5 million SLC-PREP grant. In the following sections I will share our ASP structure, funding, cultural changes, and strategies for sustainability that we used to shift school culture and ultimately transform from a failing school to a reputable, and far more equitable (though always a work in progress), institution.

Structure

As we worked together to design a program that would work for us, we traveled to Buffalo, New York to my high school alma mater City Honors School, which is currently rated in the top twenty on the list of U.S. public high schools. Despite the obstacles presented by the Buffalonian economic landscape, the school continues to reap success in terms of graduation rate, college acceptance rates, and enrollment in AP and IB programming for high school students. Above all, our trip to Buffalo proved to teachers from Portland that fruitful and impactful equity-based education was possible in a community facing dire financial adversity. We, Portlanders, needed to stop limiting our potential.

City Honors School has some features very different from Franklin High School, namely that students take an admittance test either in the fifth or ninth, so it naturally draws the most highly performing students into its safety net. Franklin is a neighborhood school with a 55% free and reduced lunch population. We, as a community of educators, did not desire the opportunity to create another barrier to excellence by creating an admissions exam—nor did we believe in this. We decided to take one facet of the City Honors model and apply it to our specific context—we wanted to shift toward a school culture of academic excellence; we wanted to create an environment where it was cool to be smart.

We created an application contract for students to sign in which they committed to take three or more AP courses before graduation. Since every single student in the program exceeded this expectation in the first year, we decided to require students to take four AP courses, or three AP courses and one Dual Credit course. We decided to focus on promoting our AP program because we had more AP options already in place, but also because, according to the College Board's research, there is a proven correlation between students taking one or more AP course and graduating from college. No such proven, researched correlation exists for Dual Credit courses yet. Also, we decided that students would be required to keep a 2.75 GPA, refrain from receiving disciplinary referrals, and have consistent attendance (85% or higher). Each student received a mentor (hopefully already one of their teachers to facilitate ease in the relationship). Mentors would help students with resumes and with the college application process both one-on-one and in after-school sessions provided throughout the year.

We were able to pay our teacher/mentors for one to two hours of additional pay per month at their hourly rate.

While this does not account for all of the supplementary social work that teachers did to aid students, it did allow teachers to earn additional money while doing what they love most—helping students to understand the path to college.

We also agreed that this would never be a punitive program. In other words, if a student falls below the 2.75 GPA requirement or earns a disciplinary referral, we had a safety net system to deal with that and help them get back on track to meet our high expectations. In this kind of scenario where a student was slipping, the mentor, the student, and I (the program coordinator) sat down to learn more about what is going on in that child's life. We did not kick the student out of the program. We were there to support them and redirect them to their collegiate goals, so much so that, most likely, a student would be expelled from school before they were officially kicked out of ASP (though this has never happened).

Mentoring

Each student who committed to the program received a mentor teacher, which helped to facilitate a teaching culture of equity as well. The high rates of student participation and success is the best defense available against the idea that "college is not for everyone."

Nationally, we know the idea that some students should, while others shouldn't, go to college becomes a statement for institutionalized racism when colleges and universities are populated, overwhelmingly, by white people. Until there is equity—meaning collegiate populations that reflect the diversity of the U.S., then the argument that only some students should go to college will always have racist undertones. At Franklin, our students represented for their right to pursue higher education. When I argue for higher education, I include both academic, career, and trade education programs—nowadays all require a college or community college education of some kind to move beyond poverty-wage jobs.

Teachers in the program acted as role models for students, but also as guardians of the idea that every student has the right and ability to earn a college degree, even if that means reaching beyond their parents' level of education. Sometimes, students don't need a teacher to work with them every day after school (there was a tutoring center to support academic needs afterschool), but they do need a caring teacher to testify publicly, by assuming the role of mentor, their belief in the student.

Mentor groups met in small groups of multi-grade students throughout the year. Each mentor group meeting has a different topic. At the start of the year, groups made three academic goals for the year, sharing them with their mentor and mentor group members. Mid-year, the groups reviewed their goals and looked at each student's level of success. At the end of the year, seniors shared their wisdom about success in high school and the college application process with younger students.

ASP Curriculum

In addition to small mentor group meetings, students attended after-school sessions on topics designed by program mentors. Teacher mentors were paid about two hours per month for the extra work they did with their mentees. Teachers who build a curriculum for large group meetings are also paid for the time they use to develop and deliver curriculum beyond the school day. The after-school curriculum is all centered around preparing students for the college application process and the reality of college. Following is an example of the yearly calendar of after-school ASP curriculum:

SEPTEMBER

Program sign-up

OCTOBER

First mentor meeting. 465 students broken into 35 groups. Topic: My Three Academic Goals for the School Year

NOVEMBER

Trip to a college campus to attend a college-level writing class and to tour the dorms. Open to all the seniors in the program.

NOVEMBER

9th/10th grade ASP students meeting in the auditorium for a presentation on preparation for AP courses and stories of resilience.

11/12th grade students meet in the gym for a presentation on the college application process.

JANUARY

9th and 10th grade - Meeting with mentors for grade checks.

11th grade - Resume building

12th grade - Financial aid and scholarships

FEBRUARY

9th and 10th graders - Meet in the auditorium for forecasting presentation: Building a Powerful Transcript

11th graders - Using Technology for SAT/ACT Prep

12th graders - Seniors meet to prepare to lead mentor groups next month

MARCH

Seniors lead ASP meeting for younger students. Topic: Success in Challenging Courses

APRIL

Mandatory mentor meeting in small mentor groups for goals check

EARLY MAY

Due to AP Exams, mentor meetings are not held during early May. Instead, all AP teachers hold afterschool study sessions. The AP Study Session calendar is given out to all ASP students. Snacks are provided in the AP study sessions.

LATE MAY

After AP exams, teachers hold a senior circle in the library. At senior circle, all mentors come down one by one, to the center of the circle to share one piece of wisdom about college.

JUNE

Final Stole Ceremony - Mandatory ALL ASP meeting. All ASP students come to the auditorium for a special event. Seniors line up

(125 total) and each senior shares with the younger students where they will be attending college and what scholarships they won. After they speak briefly, their mentor puts their silver ASP stole around their neck so that they can wear it to graduation.

Funding

In 2007–08, my fellow teacher Pam Garrett and I applied for a $2.5 million federal grant that was funded by the Gates team (called the SLC-PREP) grant to establish an equity-based program at Franklin High School. We were awarded the money, which was split between two high schools over a five year period and included salaries. This left us with approximately $100,000 per year to establish our program. We used the money to recruit more teachers to become AP trained, hold academic intervention meetings to encourage non-traditional AP students to take AP courses, and pay teachers to take on mentor groups of students who wished to participate.

After the end of our grant period, we faced a time of great fear. How would we sustain this worthwhile program? I applied to multiple grants through the NEA, as well as a program-saving $30,000 grant from the Nike School Innovation Fund, and with help from the Franklin PTSA, we stayed afloat before receiving sustainable backing from Portland Public Schools. Finally, we were able to demonstrate the success of the program to the district; the bulk of current program funding came from PPS. The Franklin PTSA and the Nike School Innovation Fund continue to support the program by donating funds for stoles and program shirts.

It is essential for more teachers to become AP trained. The NEA offers grants for teachers. Many PTSAs also offer grants to support the work of educators. Donors Choose is an excellent organization through which to seek funds. Also, each state's department of education may offer grants for teachers who wish to gain AP, IB, or STEM training. All ASP teachers are encouraged to pursue these grants and attend workshops to maintain their professional skills.

Cultural Changes

For this kind of structure to function successfully, teachers must be on-board with the concept of inclusive AP. *Inclusive AP* is a term used to describe removing barriers to AP courses that historically marginalize students living in poverty and students of color so that all students may participate at will, expanding course options that bear college credit to all students in a school population. Special education students can also be included in AP Programs (and many are included at Franklin). Students with severe vision or hearing impairments, or ADD, ADHD, or Autism, for example, need not be marginalized from stimulating courses and opportunities for higher education. Public resources, such as Braille translators and transcribers are used at Franklin to provide equal access to AP and Dual Credit courses.

As we learned at Franklin, in a school with a high F&R population, teaching inclusive AP does require additional commitment from the AP teachers. Because AP teachers work with diverse demographics that include English language learners (ELL), or ELL students who are not proficient in English but have been exited from ELL, special education students, and students who will be the first in their family to attend college, we realized that we needed to frontload all curriculum with academic language, never assuming that students have access to academic language in their homes.

For an untracked AP program to thrive, a critical mass of educators willing to create curricular plans that include all learners must be established. We had a starting group of very dedicated teachers and administrators, but we weren't done with building our community. We reached out to other teachers, administrators, the PTSA, parents who weren't in the PTSA, and any other potential allies to help build our team.

Sustainability Strategies

After we had established ASP, we learned how essential it is to continually maintain the changes in our school and spread the message about the changes. Doing so helped us gain public support for our work, and district and state officials acknowledged Franklin High School for excellent work. This recognition gave us the momentum we needed to keep moving forward and not fall back into the old patterns that were deeply entrenched. Here are some strategies for publicizing, securing, and maintaining success that we used at Franklin.

Record Successes

After two years of teaching AP in an inclusive environment, I began to notice a pattern. Students who had failed the state writing test during their sophomore year passed it in droves when they retook it in the spring after several months of AP English. I began to record these successes. When I could prove a distinct pattern, I brought this data to the principal. She was thrilled and asked for a copy so that she could share it with the other principals in the district as direct evidence supporting the philosophy that raising expectations and providing supports, especially in low-income communities and communities of color, is far more effective than archaic and discriminatory remediation systems.

Publicize Successes

As the population of students at our school taking AP courses grew, I found opportunities to share the news. An article I submitted about the diverse population of students taking AP courses at FHS was accepted for the College Board's Spotlight on Diversity publication. The author included a two-page, full-color article, along with ten other schools in the U.S. who have diverse AP populations, in a brochure that was given out to thousands of attendees at the National AP conference. The local news noticed the spotlight and came to do an article about the ASP. Each year when newspaper reporters wish to tell the stories of amazing students who have surpassed incredible obstacles to make it to college, they now know they can come to Franklin to find these remarkable stories.

The publicity makes students feel great about attending their school. Within the city of Portland, FHS became well known for a high-level of instruction, which was available in multiple disciplines; the school gained a reputation for both grit and success. This kind of publicity has a positive impact on school culture. Teachers who worked as mentors in the program took pride in their work. Wearing the program sweatshirt became a source of pride, just as one might have as part of a winning athletic team, but this pride was academic pride. If you are dealing with a history of being labeled a "failing" or "bad" school, then you must become aware of who your local journalists are, you must save your positive data and have it ready at all times. I kept a file very close to my desk and a number of accurate statistics close to my heart at all times. You will need to combat negative public perception through broadcasting success to break the spell cast by negative results of the past.

Spotlight Program Teachers

Our PTSA recognized one teacher per month with a gift card and an award at the PTSA meeting. Teachers, students, and staff members could nominate a teacher. All of the nominations were put into a hat from which the winner is drawn. Those who didn't win one month were kept in the hat to, potentially, win in the future. This system created a wonderful opportunity for staff members to share about the positive work of their peers. It also created a decisive bond between the teachers and the parents; while they appreciated the work of educators, teacher gratitude for their service grows when we see the time and energy that they are putting into recognizing us. Overall, this is excellent for morale and maintaining the culture of achievement and brilliance.

Share Expertise

Teachers worked with administrators to offer half an hour presentations at each required professional development session. The presentations showcased our teachers' expertise while also helping administrators to fill professional development time with quality material that will positively impact pedagogy. It was a win-win because teachers prefer to learn from fellow teachers. Having fellow teachers share their strategies normalizes sheltered instruction, frontloading of academic vocabulary, and student-centered teaching through strategic speaking out and sharing in staff meetings.

Focus on the Positive

Teaching, over an extended period, can go one of two ways—either you can drown in the negativity or focus your mind on the positive stories that are happening all around you. You can focus on student failure, or you can focus on the incredible *potential for success* that lies within each and every student. You can fall into the cracks in the dysfunctional system, or you can organize inside of it, all the time taking notes on how to revolutionize it. Approaching the career with a single-minded devotion to finding the potential in each human being who enters your room and refusing to stop until you unlock that potential is the cornerstone of excellent pedagogy.

Shut Down Negativity

In staff meetings, conversation sometimes opens up for educators to express disapproval or whine about students or who have given up. Some staff members viewed group meeting time, either in the staff lounge or the professional meeting setting, as a time to whine and complain about everything that is going wrong. I, and many of my colleagues at Franklin tried to shut down negativity by vocalizing alternative viewpoints. Some of us can quickly do this in the moment, but others need to prepare responses. Colleagues and I reviewed our yearly plan for professional development and had lunch together to try to brainstorm what topics or voices may come up (in schools with entrenched racism, certain individuals are often holding that negative pattern down through the way they represent themselves both in front of students and in staff meetings). Then we prepared ourselves with data and the knowledge that we as a group were willing to speak back to cynicism. Don't go into this battle alone. Afterwards, we met again to discuss how our approach could be stronger.

Keep Evidence at the Ready

Because we forged a positive relationship with an equity-focused administrator, we had access to boatloads of data that reflects that racism is endemic in our school and district. I memorized several statistics, so I had them handy when a cynic pushed back or when a reporter wanted to interview me.

Keep the Door Open

I always keep my door open for others to come to me to discuss supporting and reaching all students. Many initiatives will come down the pike to try to solve the problem of racism. This is a hundred million dollar industry. The real work and this has been true since the Civil Rights Era, will be done by educators who want to do equity work because it is their heart's calling. This is not to say that equity trainers should not be paid for educating largely white teaching staffs; it is simply that a deeper commitment is necessary, by educators of color in public schools and their white allies, to make this work viable for the long haul. Six sessions of professional development by "Equity R Us" at the rate of $60,000 per school will never be as successful as six hard-nosed, equity-bent accomplices working with positive energy and absolute dedication to solve the problems and send the message of racial justice in their schools over a long period of time. In your own mind, where would Dr. King fit into those two examples? My friends, regardless of the religion you practice, this work takes faith, love, and courage and most of all respect. Those can't be bought or sold; they must be practiced, given-freely, felt, and earned.

Keep your door open for informal mentorship. Work with your administrator to develop a formalized system of mentorship for incoming teachers where the mentor teachers are all *doing the work of equity in efforts to pass along the institutional wisdom.*

At FHS, the establishment of the Advanced Scholar Program went hand in hand with the shifting of school culture. A small group of teachers formed the program. All of the teachers agreed about the need for a powerful system of mentors to support the needs of our diverse population. The success of the program, and the demand for the program spoke for itself. Hundreds of kids signing up, on their own volition, to be mentored on the college application process affirms the immense need for the program; furthermore, it was evidence of the students' approval of the culture of inclusive AP.

Please take any of the Franklin ASP strategies that you find useful, but understand that none of them are proscriptive. Unfortunately, we know that one size fits all is absurd within the exceptionally diverse climates in U.S. public schools. Above all, please understand that teacher, student, and community-led school transformation is possible.